Marketing
for Architects
and Designers

Marketing for Architects and Designers

Harold Linton

Laura Clary

and Steven Rost

W. W. NORTON & COMPANY

NEW YORK • LONDON

To graphic designers and
visual communications specialists
who support architecture
and the allied disciplines.

For information about permission to reproduce selections from
this book, write to Permissions, W. W. Norton & Company, Inc.,
500 Fifth Avenue, New York, NY 10110

Manufacturing by KHL Printing
Book design by Gilda Hannah
Production manager: Leeann Graham

Library of Congress Cataloging-in-Publication Data

Linton, Harold.
    Marketing for architects and designers / Harold Linton, Laura
Clary, and Steven Rost.
        p. cm.
    Includes bibliographical references and index.
    ISBN 0-393-73100-6
        1. Architectural services marketing—United States. 2.
Design services—United States—Marketing. I. Clary, Laura. II.
Rost, Steven. III. Title.

NA1996.L558 2005
720′.68′8—dc22

                                                    2004057565

ISBN 0-393-73100-6

W. W. Norton & Company, Inc., 500 Fifth Avenue,
New York, N.Y. 10110
www.wwnorton.com

W. W. Norton & Company Ltd., Castle House, 75/76 Wells St.,
London W1T 3QT

0 9 8 7 6 5 4 3 2 1

Contents

Preface

Marketing for Architects and Designers is a practical sourcebook written for architects, designers, and marketing professionals who have need for a reference book of print and digital forms of marketing and communication. The purposes of marketing, advertising, and communications are changing in response to competition from national and international firms, commercial developers, and planners. In the new global economy, entrepreneurship and innovation are breeding a new generation of young architects and designers who bring a fresh outlook and a new set of values to architecture. Creative concepts for public relations and promotion instruments, in conjunction with high-end technological skills, are the means to establishing the distinctiveness of your firm.

Design communications for architecture are evolving from print to digital, static to interactive, and video to virtual. Innovations such as the Internet, Intranet, and multimedia materials raise the bar on every aspect of marketing and promotion. These innovations also keep pace with rapidly changing practices in architectural design. This book offers readers an international portfolio of current marketing instruments—be they technologically advanced or traditional—that represent leading architecture, interior design, landscape design, graphic design, and planning and development offices. We have gathered a collection of marketing materials from over fifty outstanding architecture and design firms across five continents and seventeen countries. The wealth of ideas included in this collection is diverse and inspiring. With the goal of promoting innovative visual communi-

cations and illustrating the most current concepts in marketing and graphic design, we have included richly imaginative examples of visual communications for firms both large and small, young and well-established, with great investment in the latest technology and with long-held traditional approaches to print media in marketing and promotion.

Gary L. Skog 's humorous and engaging introduction about the nature of marketing in today's architecture practice addresses the most important aspects of the complex and interrelated strategies of defining goals and objectives for marketing. This glimpse into the planning processes by one of today's most successful marketing strategists in architecture provides a basic map for the labyrinth of modern business practices and marketing-program development.

In the afterword, Weld Coxe, founding principal emeritus of the Coxe Group, the oldest and largest organization of management consultants serving architects and other professional design firms, paints a portrait of the highlights and history of marketing materials and their traditional role in the promotion of architecture. He has selected several fine examples from his collection of over 500 historic brochures and other marketing materials to illustrate his discussion of the purpose and importance of promotional materials in architecture.

Architects must remain creative and enterprising—thinking outside the box is essential in today's marketplace. It is our hope that this book will inspire you to be innovative in your marketing efforts as well.

Acknowledgments

This project could not have happened without the support of many people. We are deeply grateful to Gary L. Skog for his wit and realism, which are reflected in his superb analysis of the marketing and promotion of products and services for architecture. We are equally indebted to our colleague Weld Coxe. We first met Weld Coxe on his lecture circuit touring architecture schools in the 1980s, and we were taken not only with his wisdom and wit but also with the strength of his advocacy for the promotion of common-sense marketing and business services for architecture and the allied design professions. We are profoundly grateful to him for his friendship and for sharing his wisdom.

We wish to thank the Society for Marketing Professional Services (SMPS) for their generous advice and support, particularly Ronald D. Worth, FSMPS, CPC, Chief Executive Officer of SMPS, Roger L. Pickar, Marketing Consultant, and Veda N. Solomon, Director of Business Development/Marketing, Raimondo Construction, Fort Lee, New Jersey, who gave freely of their wisdom and expertise. We are also grateful to those architecture and design firms who supplied information regarding the price and quantity of their marketing instruments.

Special thanks are due to my coauthors, Laura Clary of HarleyEllis, in Southfield, Michigan, and Steven Rost, Associate Professor of Architecture, Lawrence Techno-logical University, in Southfield, Michigan, for their wonderful friendship. Laura and Steve's wisdom regarding the nature and significance of this project as well as their consummate artistry and technological expertise are simply irreplaceable. We would like to thank Dennis Sievers, Sievers' Photography, in Peoria, Illinois, for his superb photographic support. We wish to thank Chuck Roguske and the Presentation Center, in Troy, Michigan, for digital photographic support. We are also grateful to Eugene Nana Ekow Maison, graduate student at Bradley University, for his generous assistance with the organization of background materials and research for this book.

It would not be possible to end this note without expressing our gratitude to Nancy Green and Casey Ruble. We are grateful for their belief in the concept of a visual communications sourcebook for architecture and design. Their advice and wisdom regarding how this book could meet the needs of those in the profession are gratefully appreciated.

Nothing would have been possible, however, without the love of our families, who helped to make it possible for us to devote so much time to the research, creation, and production of this project. We are grateful to John Galuardi, Andrea Eis, and Deeni Linton for their good humor, love, and support throughout the process of yet another creative project.

Introduction
Gary L. Skog
FAIA, HarleyEllis

Erma Bombeck once wrote, "housekeeping, if done correctly, will kill you." At times I feel the same way about marketing. Thinking about all the things we should be doing or could be doing to improve our marketing efforts can be overwhelming. Are we reaching out to prospective clients enough? Are we paying enough attention to our existing customers? Are we in the right markets? Are we being published enough? Are our proposals and interviews effective? Should we advertise, and if so, where? The list seems endless.

I remember talking with the president of a fifty-person architecture firm on the West Coast. They had developed a specialty in large mixed-use projects and were designing a number of them in the Pacific Rim. When I asked him about their marketing process, he responded, "We don't believe in marketing." He then went on to explain that he had written a book on mixed-use projects, had consequently been invited to speak on the subject all around the world, and had enjoyed a stream of projects that naturally flowed from that effort. In other words, he narrowed his firm's focus to a single specialty, positioned himself as an expert in that arena, participated in target-rich events to tell his story, and became an effective enough closer to capture some very significant work. We should all "not market" that well!

I'm not advocating that we all focus on one specialty service or project type and forget the rest, but focus is certainly one key to successful marketing. The more salient point to the previous story is that, without recognizing it as marketing, this firm made some classic marketing moves to position themselves for success. They focused on a particular market segment, established themselves as experts in that area through writing and speaking opportunities, and were able to capitalize on the project leads that came from that effort.

Much has been written about marketing professional design services. A whole industry of consulting and technology firms exists to support the effort, and each one has its own take on how to approach it. Some emphasize "relationship" marketing. Some view marketing as strictly process-driven—a numbers game whereby so many contacts lead to so many requests for proposals, which lead to so many wins. Others see it as a constant effort to differentiate oneself from the competition by continually repackaging or putting a new spin on services. And some maintain that it is the perfecting of the art of proposal writing and interviewing.

As you might expect, there is some truth in all of these approaches. Relationships are certainly important. We all know it is often better and cheaper to maintain existing clients than to constantly chase new ones. But I would also argue that that is tougher to do these days. In our global marketplace, an increasing number of clients are willing and able to seek the right expertise from wherever they choose. It is also harder, given the pace of career changes, mergers, and acquisitions, to maintain personal relationships over time. This means your relationships need to be based not only on trust and friendship, but also on your ability to deliver the goods as well as everyone else.

The continual development of new clients is also important to maintaining and growing a practice. This is where understanding the science and art of marketing is important. I see the science part of marketing as the process of identifying and relating the various activities that make up the effort. The art of marketing lies in the implementation of those activities. The diagram on page 10 illustrates the overall marketing process we use at our firm and how the various marketing activities relate.

As you can see, we view the marketing process as a series of sequential activities that feed back on themselves to continually modify and improve the total effort. Notice that we include actual service delivery as a marketing activity. In fact, service delivery is probably the most important activity, because ultimately it is what your client will remember and where your staff needs to deliver. It also connects everyone in your firm to the marketing effort and establishes your "brand."

Viewing the entire marketing process this way not only allows us to feel that we are "covering the bases," but also gives us a chance to look at each component and examine how we can improve in that area. We

Marketing Process

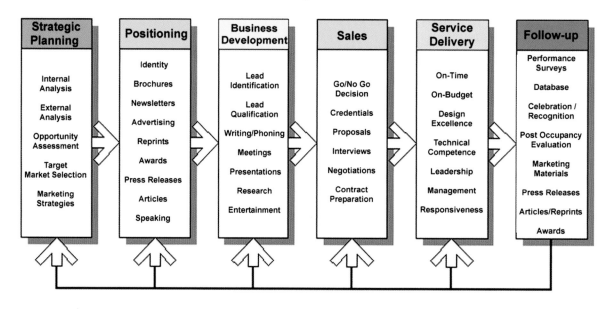

apply this process across all of our market segments independently, with each group in the firm being responsible for developing their overall strategic plan, determining how best to position themselves in their market, monitoring their business-development activities, preparing for and closing sales, delivering services, and organizing follow-up activities.

In addition to service delivery we put strong emphasis on positioning activities, particularly through speaking and writing, and encourage our lead people to participate in conferences, seminars, and industry groups within their market. Expertise sells, and there is no better way to be—and be seen as—an expert than to immerse your firm in your client's industry. This concept applies even to firms whose target expertise is design in a general sense. The best design firms view being published and speaking about design as essential to establishing and maintaining their market position.

We also play the numbers game in this process. We utilize full-time business-development managers to routinely call on new and existing clients to introduce our firm and to understand their service needs. We maintain and continually expand our client database and strive to have an interesting direct mail piece go out each month to everyone on the list. And we support these efforts with routine press releases and select, targeted advertising.

Much of the process side of marketing is pure per-sistence and legwork. But this part of the process is most effective in bringing you opportunities for work. Closing on those opportunities is where the art of marketing comes in, particularly during the request for proposal and interview stages. Many consultants argue that if you're really effective at marketing, you shouldn't have to compete for work; it should just come to you through your qualifications and relationships with clients. I find this to be a little naïve. Competition is a fact of life. Most public work requires it and many private organizations demand it. I believe it is essential to know how to compete well. It keeps you sharp and open to new ideas and approaches.

If you look at the sales part of the marketing process, it typically breaks down as a two-step effort including a written response to a request for qualifications or request for proposal followed by a live interview. Volumes of how-to books and articles have been written about each step, and whole seminars are devoted to improving our skills in preparing and delivering successful proposals and interviews, so I won't attempt to deliver my own how-to story here. Having participated on both sides of the seminar table, however, I would like to share some general observations gleaned from my thirty-year perspective.

Most responses to request for qualifications and request for proposals are far too overdone. If you have never had a chance to actually be a part of a selection committee to review twenty or more requests for qualifications for a project, I recommend you ask a trusted client to let you do so. It beats a seminar hands down. I guarantee that by the third or fourth proposal you will be brain-dead. We typically try to explain so much about the particular nuances of our firm, our team, our approach, our consultants, or some other aspect of our "pitch" that we lose sight of how little time the reviewers have (or want) to spend reading it. Recently I had a chance to be on the selection committee for a very large research facility project. We had a week to review sixteen submittals. When our eight-person committee met to discuss the submittals, at least two people had not even begun to read them and were frantically scanning the pictures at the meeting!

We need to remember we're trying to get to the interview list at this point, not capture the project. Clients only want to know if you're *qualified* enough for them to want to talk with you. The best approach is to be concise, answer their questions directly, and get to the point quickly. Simplicity of organization is important. Ease of reading is important—ten pages of single-spaced type with quarter-inch margins won't be read. Quality of photos is important. If you have directly related project experience, make sure it comes out strongly and early in the submittal.

When you make the short list for an interview, the real fun begins. And my view is that if you make it to the dance, anybody can win. There are sure to be some teams that are considered favorites, but anything can happen and usually does. You need to look at the interview as a singular event in and of itself, separate from all that went before it. A common error is to rely too much on credentials and past project experience, especially if your team has a strong position. Often the competitor without strong project experience is the one with a fresh approach. The client already knows you're qualified—that's why you're at the interview. What they really want to know is who you and your team are as individuals. They want to see what it would be like to work with you and how they would be included in the process. They want to know what you think about their project. Where are the opportunities and the challenges? They want to see some passion.

Of course, you have to do your homework. You have to know who is on the selection committee and what their hot buttons are. But you can't just throw a bunch of information at them without letting them know why the information is pertinent and what benefit they will receive. Most important, there has to be some sense of a story to it all—one that will resonate with them and capture their passion. That's where the art comes in. The kicker is that even when you win, you may not really know why. Sometimes it's a word, an expression, a picture, or just the fact that they like you.

Maybe Erma was right.

1. Corporate Identity Packages

Branding, the consistent use of identity art on marketing instruments, fosters recognition of your architecture and design firm within the public sector. Key to branding is your firm's identity package, which should include a logo design with the firm's name and contact information and a flexible set of business materials such as stationery, envelopes, business cards, memo forms, and business forms. All of these materials are enclosed in a bifolder or trifolder whose design strategy adheres to that of the firm's identity program. The firm's brochure is also often included in the folder and incorporates the graphic elements found in the identity package.

The identity package plays an important role in establishing your firm's profile throughout the processes of client prospecting, client acquisition, design communications, management, and follow-through, suggesting at all stages a high level of organization, refinement, and accomplishment. Because the identity package so strongly influences a prospective client's first impression of a firm, it should clearly convey the firm's niche in the market. This in turn enables your firm to be considered as a specialist for a given project.

Large firms often contract graphic design firms or an accomplished visual communications specialist to design their logo and identity package. Medium-sized and small firms may have someone in-house with a visual communications background and significant experience in logo and identity package design. Once the designs are created and approved by the partners of the firm, the logo design and identity graphics can be applied to almost all of the print materials and digital products of the firm.

Firm Names and Tag Lines

Architecture and design firms often adopt acronyms derived from the first initials of the last names of the founding principals or partners. These acronyms can be used in the logo design and name of the firm.

Firms with a long history of practice often retain the name or names of the original founding partners to highlight the legacy of the firm. Sometimes, if the firm's size is medium or small, the last name of the owner is used as the name of the firm. Occasionally, if the firm is focused on a specific philosophy, such as experimental or innovative design, the firm's name includes the main focus of the services being offered, such as Lab architecture studio or Creative Logic, Inc.

Firms also often include a tag line, a phrase that identifies the firm, in their identity package and logo design. Tag lines broaden the logo and synthesize the mission, philosophy, or professional specialization of the firm. For example, TVS (Thompson, Ventulett, Stainback & Associates) uses the phrase "Turning Possibilities Into Realities." The Olin Partnership's tag line is: "Powerful Concepts, Beautiful Solutions, Elegantly Made."

Logos

The logo is among the most important elements of the identity package and should relate to the other parts of the package. It is wise to explore a range of graphic images to determine what will best represent your firm's overall branding goals. Do you wish to convey an informal, friendly image or one that is more formal and restrained? Do you want to communicate your firm's focus on high technology and innovation or present an image of historic precedence and sobriety?

A high-quality visual image should be established for the logo early in your firm's history and remain consistent throughout all facets of correspondence and communication where the company name is involved. Logos can be featured on all official documents, corporate stationery, and proposal presentation material. Your firm's identification as well as all components of your firm's print package—stationery, forms, newsletters, brochures, folders and covers, and drawings—should carry the logo and associated graphics. Redesign of a firm's old logo can help alert clients to upgrades in the company and reflect growth and expansion of services. Figure 1.1 shows a wide range of logos from many of the firms featured in this book. A variety of logos developed for design firms by

gmp

RossDrulisCusenbery

Loebl Schlossman & Hackl
Architecture · Planning · Interiors

MURPHYMEARS
Architects

GRAHAM GUND ARCHITECTS

SMWM

J|C|Y

il KAJIMA DESIGN

RAY +
HOLLINGTON
architects

h+k

KPF

LEVY DESIGN PARTNERS

Architects and Planning Consultants
New York, London, Tokyo

SheppardRobson

ARCHITECTURE   INTERIORS   URBAN DESIGN   PLANNING

BENTEL ABRAMSON & PARTNERS
ARCHITECTURE • INTERIOR DESIGN • GRAPHIC DESIGN

ARCHITECTURE

GORDON H CHONG
& Partners

SmithGroup JJR

evata

Cambridge Seven Associates, Inc.

K *Karlsberger*

murray**ō**laoire architects

joehnk.

Interior Design

CHETWOOD associates

...enwell Green, London, EC1R 0QJ

...Caroline St, Birmingham, B3 1TR

Tel 020 7490 2400

Tel 0121 234 7500

ATELIER D'ART URBAIN

A R C H I T E C T S

tvs

OlinPartnership

HARLEY ELLIS

Creative Logic, Inc., in Peoria, Illinois, are compiled in the company's *Big Book of Logos* (figures 1.2–1.4).

The typeface and color, simplicity or complexity, and style of the logo, derived from letterform, abstract shape, and geometric form, are just a few of the ways you to communicate the identity of your firm. Kajima Design in Tokyo, Japan, uses a graphic transformation of the letter *K*'s edges to suggest the multifaceted nature of their architecture and design firm (figure 1.5). An architecture firm in Rotterdam, the Netherlands, eea (erick van egeraat associated architects), combines hot color, lowercase lettering, and suggestive

1.2. The cover of Creative Logic, Inc.'s *Big Book of Logos* showcases Creative Logic, Inc.'s own logo. Quantity: 12 books; cost: $300 each.

1.3. *Big Book of Logos* (title page).

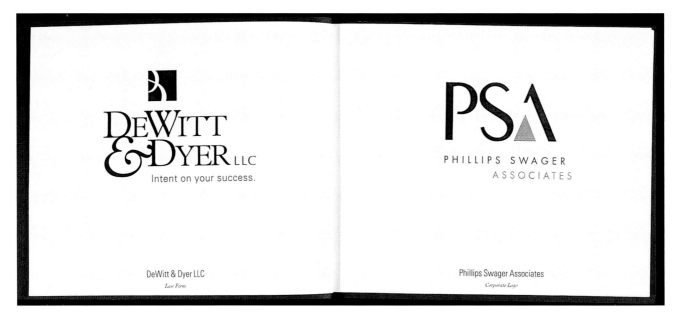

1.4. Logo designs from *Big Book of Logos.*

abstract photography to alert clients to the nature of their highly conceptual design activities across a range of in-house disciplines including architecture, interior design, and graphic design (figures 1.6, 1.7).

Once a logo has been developed and approved by your firm, you can submit it to the federal government trademark office for trademark registration approval (www.uspto.gov/teas).

Business Cards, Envelopes, Stationery, and Related Business Documents
Business cards, envelopes, stationery, and related business documents are essential ingredients of the iden-

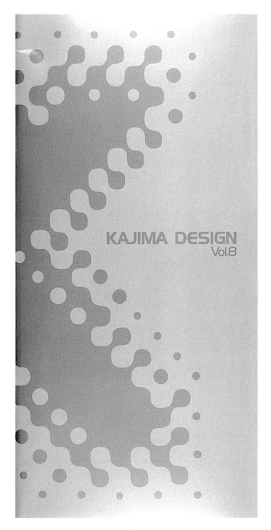

1.5. The cover of this office brochure for Kajima Design incorporates the firm's logo.

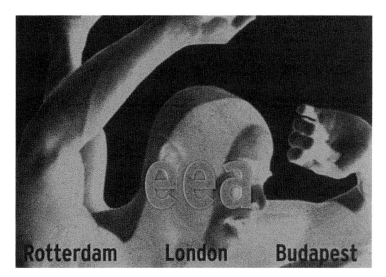

1.6. Logo for eea (erick van egeraat associated architects), seen here on an office review trifold flyer. Quantity: 500 cards; cost: 1,000 euros.

1.7. Trifold flyer (open) for eea.

tity package, and the logo design should be integrated with them. Various graphic design elements can serve as a visual metaphor for the philosophy and guiding design principles of your firm.

A firm's graphic identity is usually conveyed through typography; however, typographic forms are often imaginatively combined with colors, textures, shapes, illustrations, and photography to enliven the layout of business cards, envelopes, stationery, business forms, and brochures. For example, stability, experience, and refinement could be suggested through a conservative serif typeface, neutral colors, and traditional photography, whereas a more cutting-edge identity could be conveyed by a trendy sans serif type, saturated colors, and abstract imagery. Graphics and photography extend identity art into a rich visual experience and more fully represent the image of a firm.

Paper quality and page design also convey the image of your firm. A traditional firm with a long-standing reputation might choose heavy,

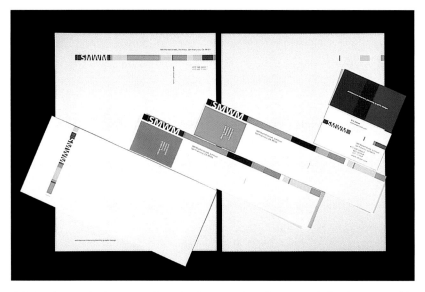

1.8. Stationery, business envelope, business card, and note cards for SMWM Architects by Tenazas Design.

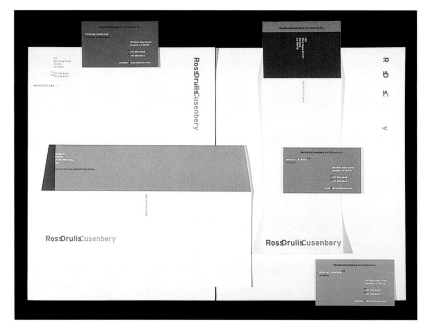

1.9. Identity package for RossDrulisCusenbery Architects Inc. by Tenazas Design.

watermarked bond paper and a dignified page design. A less traditional firm wishing to present itself as an innovator might opt for free use of color, an open composition and page design, and unconventional types, sizes, and shapes of paper.

Figures 1.8–1.12 show various elements of design packages developed by Tenazas Design of San Francisco, California, which provides graphic solutions and product design for a number of significant West Coast and national architecture firms. For SMWM Architects, in San Francisco, the firm created the stationery, business envelope, business card, and note cards shown in figure 1.8. The bar of colors incorporated in the logo and identity package suggests move-ment, and the active spatial arrangement of type and color creates a hierarchy of visual elements on the page.

The identity package for Ross-DrulisCusenbery Architecture, Inc., in Sonoma, California, uses overlapping type to convey unity among the partners of the firm and color to distinguish the names and suggest that they are of equal importance (figure

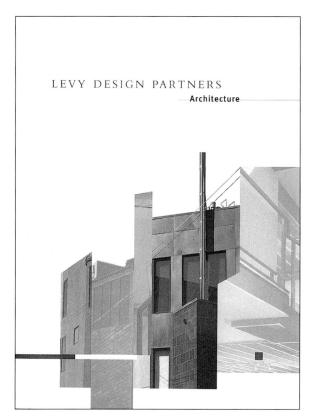

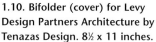

1.10. Bifolder (cover) for Levy Design Partners Architecture by Tenazas Design. 8½ x 11 inches.

1.11. Marketing identity package for Levy Design Partners Architecture by Tenazas Design.

1.9). The unconventional gray flap on the envelope coordinates with the business card and other elements to create surprise and intrigue.

The bifolder cover and business materials for Levy Design Partners Architecture, in San Francisco, are integrated through color, placement of typographical elements, and abstract graphic imagery (figures 1.10, 1.11). The colors used on the cover are repeated on the envelope, stationery, and business card, and the geometric abstract imagery on those materials mirrors the perspectival arrangement of the buildings illustrated on the bifolder. The typography, with the word "architecture" placed at a slant from the firm's name, suggests the right angle of a building's corner. The photographic montage on the cover depicts a variety of building materials and architectural facades, evoking the firm's broad design experience and range of services.

The clean minimalism of modernist architecture forms the basis for the graphic strategy behind the identity package for Gordon H. Chong & Partners, also in San Francisco (figure 1.12). The bifold cover relies heavily on the photographic qualities

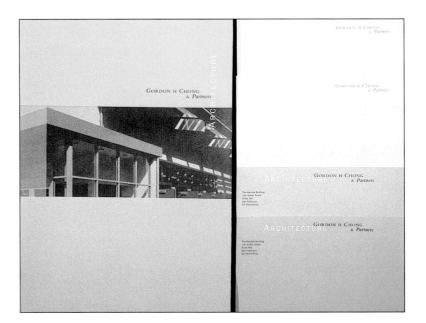

1.12. Identity package for Gordon H. Chong & Partners by Tenazas Design.

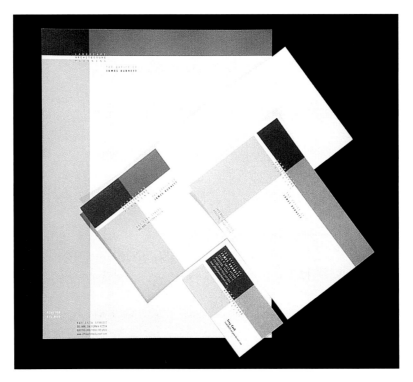

1.13. Stationery, envelope, business card, and note card for the Office of James Burnett by Minor Design Group. Quantity: 2,000; cost: $7,500; 2001.

of light, shadow, and form, and the black-and-white imagery is offset sharply with vivid yellow on the note and memo cards.

The straightforward, elegant design of the business materials for the Office of James Burnett, in Houston, Texas, developed by the Minor Design Group, also in Houston, suggests organization and accomplishment (figure 1.13). The use of the firm's full title, "The Office of James Burnett," sets a formal tone, as does the restrained color palette. The planes of color fit neatly and precisely against one another and the distinguished type layout highlights the firm's focus on planning and design.

Figure 1.14 shows how a logo can be toyed with throughout the materials of the identity package. Designed by the Minor Design Group for MurphyMears Architects, in Houston, the logo combines serif and sans serif type to create a simple yet elegant letterform in a playful organization of line and space. On the stationery and envelope the combination of the serif and sans serif types is integrated, while on the note cards the logo is split, with the sans serif type serving as the main logo and the serif type working as a graphic element on the right-hand side of the page.

The logo and identity package for Ray + Hollington architects, also in Houston, includes an asymmetrical balanced arrangement of visual elements with careful typographic composition and use of negative space (figure 1.15).

1.14. Stationery, business envelope, business card, and note card for MurphyMears Architects by Minor Design Group. Quantity: 2,500; cost: $11,000; 2000.

Brochures

Although not technically considered part of the identity package, a firm's brochure is often included in the bifolder or trifolder and is a vehicle for further dissemination of the graphic identity established by the materials in the identity package. Brochures may range in size from a single page to many pages and vary in content depending on the needs of a firm at a particular time. Some brochures serve as general advertisements for the firm; others may focus on a particular event or recent project. Brochures are generally used as part of the direct mail program, which is discussed in chapter 2.

Figures 1.15 and 1.16 illustrate identity packages for Ray + Hollington and Synectics Group Architecture Studio, in Houston. Similarities in typography and layout can be seen between the envelope, card, flyer, and brochure. The Minor Design Group, which developed this package, used finish-material textures such as birds-eye maple as design fields to lend the suggestion of material quality to the brochures.

The brochure for Baum Thornley, in San Francisco, California, uses vellum overlays to convey the firm's

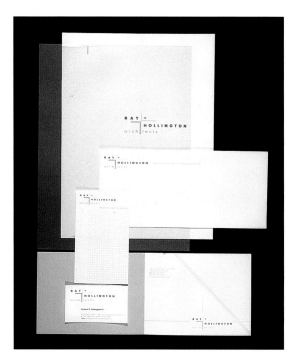

1.15. Stationery, business envelope, business card, and note card for Ray + Hollington architects by Minor Design Group. Quantity: 5000; cost: $9,000; 2000.

1.16. Envelope and self-addressed label with a small concertina flyer and bifold brochure for Synectics Group Architecture Studio by Minor Design Group. Flyer 4 x 4 inches, bifold brochure 8 x 8 inches. Quantity: 1,000; cost: $6500; 1999.

dual focus on form and function (figures 1.17, 1.18); the transparency gives otherwise cold, impersonal imagery a friendlier, lived-in feel. Printed graphics on vellum in coordination with printed graphics on the white paper beneath make a rich statement of transparent color effects, textures, and intelligent typographic presentation.

The HarleyEllis logo is an excellent example of how a logo can be used to alert clients to changes in the firm (figure 1.19). After the two firms of Harley and Ellis merged, the logo was redesigned to incorporate both names. The elimination of a portion of the letter Y suggests fluidity, while the difference in color distinguishes the two names. The colors are symbolic: reserved gray typical of the commercial business environment and purple, trumpeting a passion for design. The logo prominently appears on the cover of each department bifolder. The bifolder cover designs suggest a window into a multifaceted firm with numerous departments and business activities. The bifolder cover designs are repeated in the brochure pictured in figures 1.19–1.21.

The eea (erick van egeraat associ-

1.17. Office brochure for Baum Thornley incorporating imagery and type printed on vellum by Tenazas Design. 8½ x 11 inches.

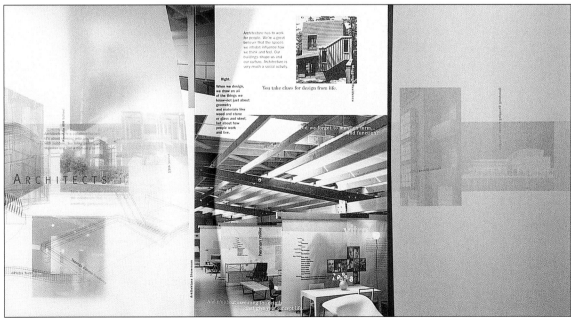

1.18. Office brochure (interior spread) for Baum Thornley.

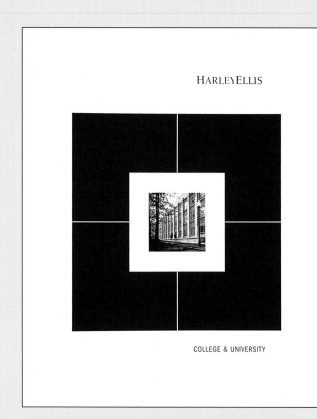

COLLEGE & UNIVERSITY

1.19. "College and University" page of trifold brochure for HarleyEllis. 8½ x 11 inches. Quantity: 2,500; cost: $6,000, 2001–2002.

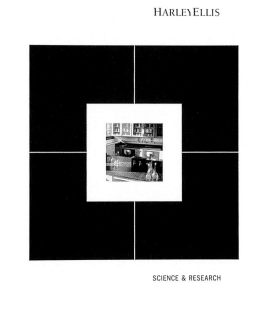

SCIENCE & RESEARCH

1.20. "Science and Research" page of trifold brochure for HarleyEllis.

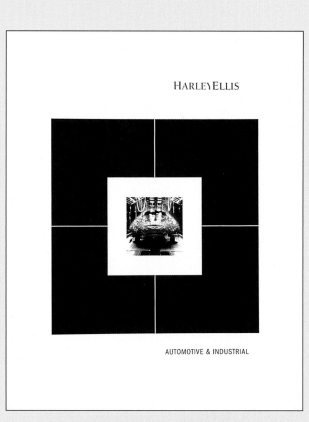

AUTOMOTIVE & INDUSTRIAL

1.21. "Automotive and Industrial" page of trifold brochure for HarleyEllis.

ated architects) office staff flyer and logo uses as visual elements lowercase type and the office-family portrait to express a creative flare and less traditional working environment (figure 1.22). The typographic layout of one name after the next with equal space between the words conveys an impression that staff are at ease and comfortable in a collegial office environment.

Bentel Abramson & Partners, an architecture, interior design, and graphic design firm in Houghton, South Africa, created a logo and identity campaign with a global image that helps to communicate the international size and scope of their practice (figure 1.23). The wire-bound and embossed silver brochure with the firm logo presents the history, philosophy, partners, accomplishments, goals, and awards of the firm. The brochure includes a com-

Agnes Szabó Akki Colenbrander Ákos Ignác Ginder Alasdair Ross Graham Alberte Harmsen Alejandra Guerra Navarro Alexander Tauber Anja Blumert Anke Schiemann Ann-Christin Hillebrand Anoeska Schipper Aude de Broissia Aylin Jorgensen-Dahl Barbara Frei Bas de Haan Bora Ilhan Boris Zeisser Bosan Bosanic Brenda Kamphuis Carla van Dijk Catrin Schall Chantal Könning Christian Nicolas Cindy Mentink Claire Booth Cock Peterse Daniël Vlasveld David Hills Dirk Schonkeren Elizabeth Grace Erick van Egeraat Erik Workel Eszter Bódi Florent Rougemont Frank Huibers Gaston Zahr Gerben Vos Gerwen van der Linden Hana Sejvlová Harry Kurzhals Harry Pasterkamp Ilse Castermans Jan Bouchal János Tiba Jeanne Lev Jeroen ter Haar Jerry van Veldhuizen Jesse Treurniet José Luis Berrueta Julia Hausmann Julia Schleppe Katrin Grubert Kliment Grozdanov Krista McLean Kristjan Kaltenbach Luc Reyn Maartje Lammers Madelene Doolaard Marc van Gompel Marcel Turic Marcela Parra Marieke Nagelkerke Mark Eacott Martine van der Berg Marylse van Bijleveld Massimo Bertolano Michael Rushe Michel van der Kar Michiel Raaphorst Monica Adams Monika Csopák Monique Voogd Paul Blonk Peter Földi Peter Heavens Petra Rudloff Ralph van Mameren Rebecca Greenfield Reinoud Nuijten Remco Boorsma Rhys Wynne Rolf van Gils Ronald Ubels Roos Kemna Rowan van Wely Sonja Bergau Stephan Jentsch Steven Simons Suzanne Toth-Pal Ulf Hackauf Wolfram Schneider Zita Balajti Zoltán Gyüre Zoltán Király Zsófia Bálint Zuzana Mertliková

2001

erick van egeraat associated architects
eea
ROTTERDAM LONDON BUDAPEST PRAGUE

1.22. Office staff trifold flyer for eea (erick van egeraat associated architects). 5¼ x 5 inches.

1.23. Logo design incorporated on brochure, CD, and CD insert for Bentel Abramson & Partners. 8½ x 11 inches.

plete portfolio of the firm's significant projects on CD.

Architectus™, in North Sydney, Australia, is an award-winning design firm concerned with sustainable principles in design (figures 1.24, 1.25). Their identity is carried over into the firm's profile brochure and incorporates monochromatic color scales in gray-blue, evoking their interest in the qualities of light, water, and the environment.

BDP (Building Design Partnership), in London, England, has created a multinational identity for their retail design company. A color bar code is transformed into a shopping bag for the brochure cover and cleverly reinterpreted inside the brochure in the form of columns of text in different languages (figures 1.26–1.28).

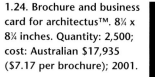

1.24. Brochure and business card for architectus™. 8¼ x 8¼ inches. Quantity: 2,500; cost: Australian $17,935 ($7.17 per brochure); 2001.

1.25. Brochure (double-page spread) for architectus™.

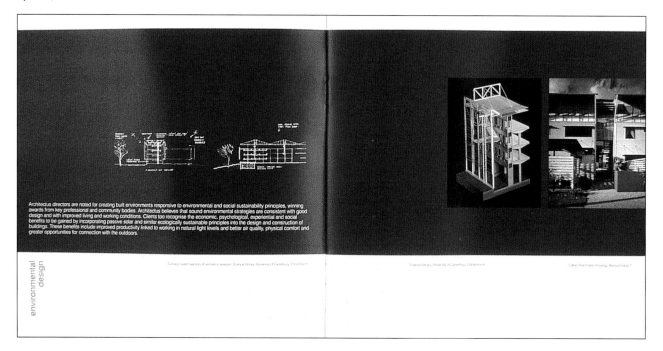

BDP's retail specialists are also introduced with brief biographies and photographs in the same sequence as the color bars on the cover and in the text.

The brochures of KPF (Kohn Pedersen Fox) Architects and Planning Consultants, in New York City, profile selected clients and projects broken down into the firm's corporate departments of architecture and planning, transportation, and interiors (figures 1.29–1.36). A classic type style combined with high-tech color and a metallic silver-gray finish suggests the firm's position as an established and accomplished design office.

1.26. Brochure (cover) for BDP (Building Design Partnership). 11¾ x 8½ inches. Quantity: 2,500; cost: £15,000; 2000.

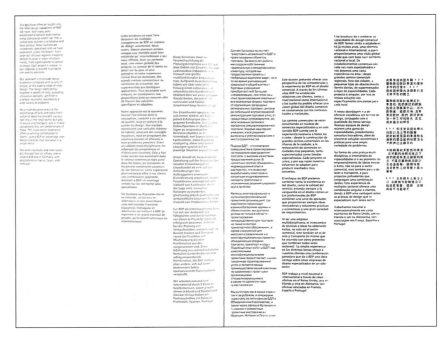

1.27. Layout design of brochure for BDP.

1.28. Color and photography extend and reinterpret BDP's identity.

1.29. Four-panel brochure (cover) for KPF (Kohn Pedersen Fox) Architects and Planning Consultants. 11¾ x 8¼ inches. Quantity: 5,000; cost: $7,800; 2000.

1.30. Four-panel brochure (interior spread) for KPF.

1.31. Four-panel brochure (inte

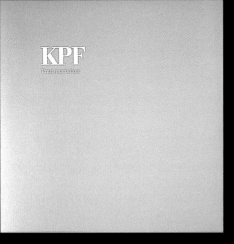

1.32. Four-panel brochure (cover) for KPF. 8¼ x 8¼ inches. Quantity: 1,000; cost: $3,300; 2000.

Kohn Pedersen Fox Associates provides full architectural and planning services for a variety of transportation and transportation-inclusive projects. Our international portfolio includes airport passenger terminal facilities, high-speed rail hubs, commuter rail stations, underground stations, ferry terminals and pedestrian bridges.

Our primary responsibility is to create highly efficient facilities that enhance the quality of the individual passenger experience. We produce designs that best utilize intuitive space programming, dynamic forms, and natural light while achieving a high level of sustainability, flexibility, and maintainability.

Our strong management methodology ensures the fulfillment of this intent. The commitment and competence of our partners and staff during all stages of the process ensures that each project is capably realized with the strictest attention to our client's budget and schedule.

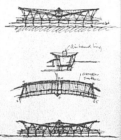

1.33. Four-panel brochure (interior spread) for KPF.

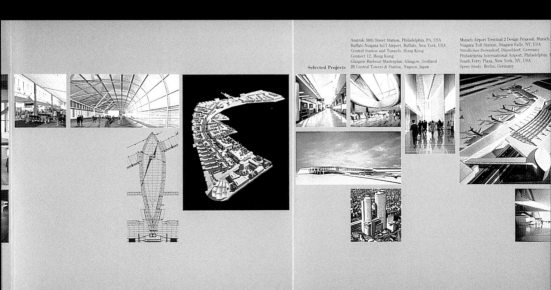

Selected Projects: Amtrak 30th Street Station, Philadelphia, PA, USA; Buffalo Niagara Int'l Airport, Buffalo, New York, USA; Central Station and Tunnels, Hong Kong; Connect 12, Hong Kong; Glasgow Harbour Masterplan, Glasgow, Scotland; JR Central Towers & Station, Nagoya, Japan; Munich Airport Terminal 2 Design Proposal, Munich; Niagara Toll Station, Niagara Falls, NY, USA; Nördliches Derendorf, Düsseldorf, Germany; Philadelphia International Airport, Philadelphia, PA; South Ferry Plaza, New York, NY, USA; Spree Study, Berlin, Germany

1.34. Four-panel brochure (interior spread) for KPF.

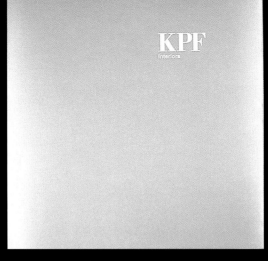

1.35. Four-panel brochure (cover) for KPF. 8¼ x 8¼ inches. Quantity: 1,000; cost: $3,300; 1999.

Kohn Pedersen Fox is an integrated architecture, planning and interior design firm whose work has been recognised globally for excellence in design in America and Europe. Since its founding in 1976 in New York, the firm has opened an office in London and expanded its work in over 30 countries. The innovative designs of the firm have helped shape the debate about the direction of architecture all over the world.

As **Architects** we help clients to realise exciting projects within stringent cost and time constraints. With these clients, we are looking beyond the construction phase in order to refine lifecycle costs, develop strategies for energy reduction and improve the quality of the user's environment. Vision enables and amplifies success.

As **Interior Designers** we create solutions which capture the spirit and identity of our clients. We include the client as a full member of the design team. We take advantage of our multinational operations to transfer knowledge and experience across the globe, thus keeping up to date with changing technologies and ideas for the workplace. Success derives from experience, competence, creativity and the uncompromising commitment to quality.

As **Space Planners**, we provide dynamic solutions which assist people to work effectively and productively. Space planning should provide environments which foster productivity, inspire the user and reinforce the spirit of the company. We ensure the optimum use of space by analysing our client's current and future requirements as well as their management and working practices. Strategic space management with innovative design motivates staff and thereby generates revenue.

1.36. Four-panel brochure (interior spread) for KPF.

2. Direct Mail: Print Communications

Direct mail as a part of brand communication traditionally consists of the printed material used to raise awareness of a firm and market its products and services. It comprises postcards, newsletters, office tear sheets, flyers, and brochures. Direct mail should convey its message in as few words and images as possible in order to attract the recipients' interest, and it should be visually compelling in order to hold their attention. As marketing professionals often profess, simplicity is the essence of elegant and effective communication. Clarity of purpose in direct-mail marketing is an integral part of finding new clients and design commission opportunities.

Direct mail entails a creative integration of advertising, public relations, and sales promotion. It relies on artwork and copy to get and keep a reader's attention, while performing public relations services and conveying a direct message. For architecture and design firms, the direct-mail concept is not based on a one-time product offer or brand advertising, but rather on a long-term dialogue with professionals who have needs and interests in good design performance.

If the content does not fit the prospective client's needs, the direct mail piece is usually quickly discarded. Keep these guidelines in mind as you manage the content of your direct mail materials:

• Text or copy must be concise, believable, personable, and easy to read. The tone should be conversational and friendly.

• Persuasive case history information should be provided. Include accurate facts, numbers, histories, or endorsements.

• The benefits of your approach or product should be enumerated, and the value of your services should be clear.

Give top priority to proper targeting and database creation for direct mail. Computers have had a huge impact on mail campaigns. They afford the opportunity to track lists, monitor responses, and use staff efficiently, saving time and money. Lists can be merged, coded, and organized by name, zip code, and region, and can be purchased and assembled in a number of ways. Professional societies and organizations such as developers, public and private institution administrators, trustees, professional consultants, and the financial sector are all available either through membership in their organizations, through associate member status, or through rental of their lists. Architectural offices also build lists by encouraging staff to report the names and contact information of those new prospects in the area. Brokers in every area of the country rent lists.

The many professional societies, organizations, conferences, and conventions throughout the country make for a readily available source of up-to-date prospect lists, which are usually accessible to firms on a rental basis. If your budget affords you the opportunity to personalize the presentation, opt for this tactic on the first approach.

Postcards

Direct mail should target clients from whom you would like to have a response and should use concise, convincing words that communicate quickly, precisely, and clearly. HOK (Hellmuth, Obata + Kassabaum), in St. Louis, Missouri, uses postcards with the phrase "Faster, Better, Smarter" to create awareness of brand, recent projects, and advances in office activities and technology applications (figure 2.1). The series of postcards used by HarleyEllis, in Southfield, Michigan, cleverly employs the alphabet and implies the phrase "from A to Z," to build clients' anticipation as they wait to receive the next piece (figure 2.2).

Studio Granda, a relatively small firm in Reykjavik, Iceland, uses beautiful photography of office projects on postcards for holidays and frequent mailings throughout the year to reinforce awareness of the firm's activities and accomplishments (figure

2.3). Loebl Schlossman & Hackl, in Chicago, Illinois, creates postcards that build awareness for each of their departments—interior design, corporate design, healthcare design, and education design (figure 2.4). They also mail calendars with images of important projects.

Postcards can be linked to other forms of direct mail through graphic design to reinforce branding and create a broader foundation of service and product awareness. Figures 2.5 and 2.6 show large-format postcards that play with the words "Questions, Choices, Solutions" in various orders to create awareness of the capabilities and problem-solving expertise of

2.1. Postcards for HOK (Hellmuth, Obata + Kassabaum). 3¼ x 9 inches. Quantity: three cards, 2,500 each; cost: $10,000; 2002.

2.2. "A to Z" project postcards for HarleyEllis. 4¼ x 6 inches. Quantity: 1,000 each; cost: $163 per thousand; 2001–2003.

2.3. Office project postcards for Studio Granda. 4 x 6 inches. Quantity: 150–500; cost: $1 per card; 1987–2002.

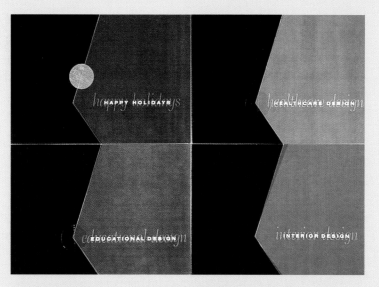

2.4. Corporate sector postcards for Loebl Schlossman & Hackl. 5 x 7 inches. Quantity: 2,000; cost: $1.19 per unit.

2.5. "Questions, Choices, Solutions" postcards (front side) for Karlsberger. 5¾ x 8¾ inches. Quantity: 2,000; cost: $2,600.

2.6. "Questions, Choices, Solutions" postcards (reverse side) for Karlsberger.

Karlsberger, in Columbus, Ohio. Another example of this concept can be found in the "Mission Critical Marketing" concept, used on postcards as well as on other forms of marketing materials by Ellerbe Becket, in Minneapolis, Minnesota (figure 2.7).

Newsletters

Typically one or two pages on a single sheet of paper that may be folded or mailed in an envelope, newsletters are a strong and enduring element of direct-mail marketing for architecture and design firms. They are fast and economical to produce. They lend themselves perfectly to simple and informative communication. The newsletter provides bite-sized articles that clients can review at their leisure to keep up to date with recent events and accomplishments in the design community.

Newsletters are also useful for in-house communication, financial summaries, technical applications, and office activity summary purposes. *Update*, from Nightingale Associates in Oxford, England, informs both clients and staff about the firm's numerous activities, competition awards, design accomplishments, and business developments (figure 2.8). The quarterly newsletter of Kajima Design, in Tokyo, Japan, tells clients of design activities across var-

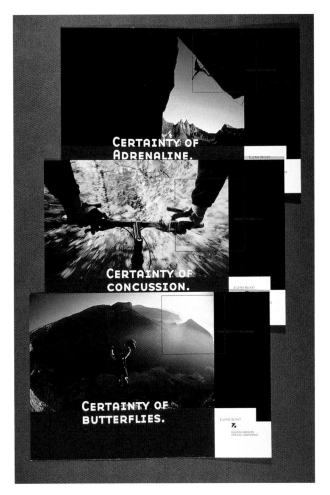

2.7. "Mission Critical Marketing" postcards for Ellerbe Becket. 6 x 9 inches.

2.8. *Update* newsletter for Nightingale Associates. 8½ x 11 inches. Quantity: 2,000; cost: £1,900; 2001, 2002.

ious sectors of this multidimensional firm and is equally useful for internal communications with the firm's large staff (figures 2.9, 2.10).

The subject matter of newsletters should be linked to the firm's objectives and its assessment of the current market for professional design services. The thrust of the firm—for example, health facilities, manufacturing facilities, or schools—will dictate what types of articles, information, and visuals to focus on. Fanning/Howey Associates, Inc., in Celina, Ohio, creates provocative newsletters with strong photographic appeal that focus on school sector specialization to raise awareness of the firm's expertise in this area of design (figure 2.11).

2.9. Newsletters (covers) for Kajima Design. 11¾ x 6 inches.

2.10. Newsletter (interior spread) for Kajima Design.

2.11. Newsletters for Fanning/Howey Associates, Inc. 8½ x 11 inches. Quantity: 2,000; cost: $11,319; 1999.

2.12. Project tear sheet for Nightingale Associates announcing completion of the Royal Berkshire Hospital. 8½ x 11 inches.

2.13. Project tear sheet for Nightingale Associates announcing completion of the Homerton Hospital. 8½ x 11 inches.

2.14. Project tear sheet for Nightingale Associates announcing completion of the Darent Valley Hospital. 8½ x 11 inches.

Tear Sheets

Project tear sheets offer a background summary of useful facts and information pertaining to the successful accomplishment of a distinguished project in the most attractive way possible. They are intentionally concise descriptions with graphics of particular projects and provide clients with a capsule version of the essential attributes of a design project.

The project tear sheets from Nightingale Associates shown in figures 2.12–2.14 announce recently completed commissions with dramatic photography and give specifics about the architecture firm. Architectus™, in North Sydney, Australia, produces several tear sheets focusing on new directions, award-winning projects, and an office overview for external marketing presentations (figures 2.15, 2.16). The office tear sheets in figures 2.17–2.19, by evata, in Helsinki, Finland, describe recent partnerships, healthcare facility design, and the firm's promise of "Commit-

2.15. "New directions" tear sheet for architectus™.
8¼ x 11¾ inches.

2.16. "Winning projects" tear sheet for architectus™.
8¼ x 11¾ inches.

2.17. "Commitment, Consistency, Communication" tear sheet for evata. 8½ x 11 inches. Quantity: as needed; cost: $0.14 per unit, printed in-house (laser printer).

2.18. "Global alliance" tear sheet for evata. 8½ x 11 inches.

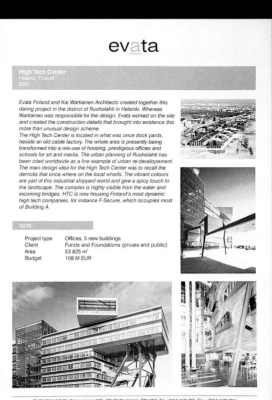

2.19. "High Tech Center" tear sheet for evata. 8 ½ x 11 inches.

ment, Consistency, Communication."

If a firm's tear sheets are designed in a consistent manner, they can be easily assembled into a firm portfolio.

Flyers and Small Brochures

Individual large and small offices engage clients and colleagues with visually stimulating direct-mail flyers to stimulate awareness and interest in the firm. Multi-page flyers or small brochures can be self-mailers (postage and address labels can be affixed to them directly) or placed inside an envelope for bulk mailing.

A holiday greeting bifold flyer from eea (erick van egeraat associated architects) uses a playful design that integrates photography and typography in a dynamic composition (figure 2.20); another eea flyer focuses on recent projects to raise awareness and draw attention to successful office commissions (figure 2.21).

Flyers may take several forms. A single page with text is common. Also popular are folded flyers that serve as holiday greetings or announce a new office location or competition result. Murrayolaoire architects, in Dublin, Ireland, uses color photography in a four-panel flyer to illustrate successful projects in multiple sectors of the

2.20. "2002 happy new year" flyer for eea (erick van egeraat associated architects). 5¼ x 5 inches. Quantity: 1,000 cards; cost: 900 euros; 2001.

2.21. Office projects flyer for eea. 5¼ x 5 inches.

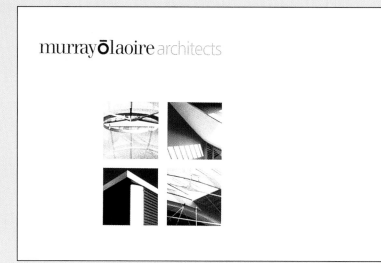

2.22. Four-panel flyer (cover)
for murrayolaoire architects.
4½ x 11 inches. Quantity:
1,000; cost: 2017 euros.

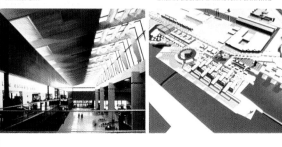

2.23. Four-panel flyer (interior
spread) for murrayolaoire architects.
8 x 17 inches.

market—cultural, industrial, housing, government, transportation, and urban planning (figures 2.22, 2.23).

Karlsberger, another multi-specialty firm, mails small flyer-brochures of a few pages each (figures 2.24, 2.25). These highlight the diversity and talents of the office staff and designers and draw attention to the varied departments within the firm.

In summary, a printed self-mailer or brochure in an envelope can be the difference in winning a job. If your mailing piece looks like "junk mail," it will be promptly discarded; if its design and content invites the recipient to open and peruse it, you may gain a new client.

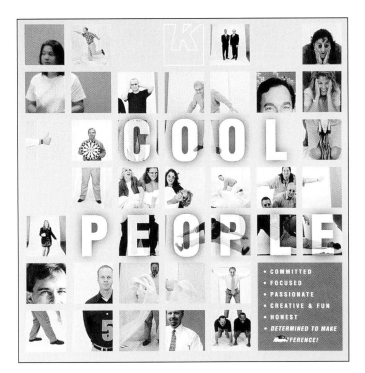

2.24 "Cool People" flyer for Karlsberger. 8 x 8 inches. Quantity: 6,300; cost: $3,600.

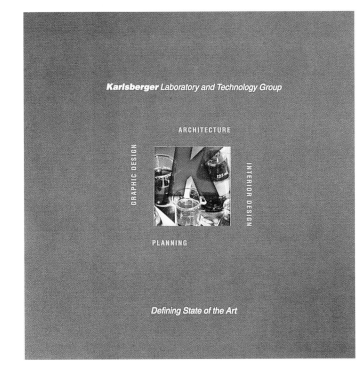

2.25. "Laboratory and Technology Group" flyer for Karlsberger. 8 x 8 inches. Quantity: 3,500; cost: $6,700.

3. Digital and Time-Based Communications

The computer has revolutionized information technology and reinvented marketing in two important ways. First, it has made the design and production of marketing pieces much easier by facilitating the assimilation, manipulation, and even creation of images, text, and graphics.

Second, digital technology has provided a new means of delivery for marketing communications in the form of the Internet, videotape, CD, and DVD. The advantages of using electronic media in marketing and delivery include significant quality control, flexibility and efficiency in

graphic design, ease of editing, and instantaneous communication of the images and messages anywhere in the world. The examples illustrated in this section are instructive to see online; the URLs current at the time of publication are listed in Appendix B.

Gmp (von Gerkan, Marg und Part-

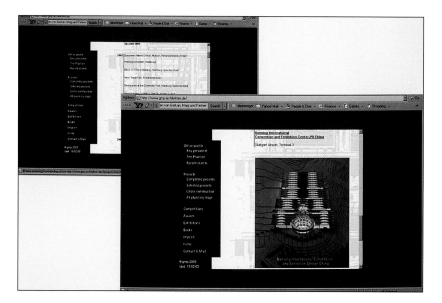

3.1. Web site for gmp (von Gerkan, Marg und Partner Architects) (www.gmp-architekten.de); cost: 30,000 euros.

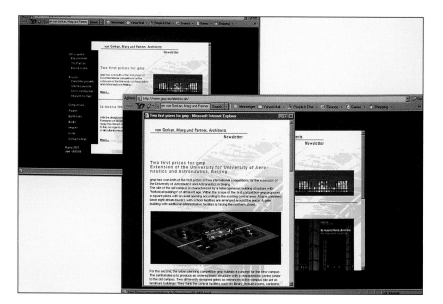

3.2. Internet-distributed office newsletter for gmp.

ner Architects), in Hamburg, Germany, makes full use of digital media in architecture and design. The gmp Web site uses text and visuals to communicate planning for a convention and exhibition hall in China (figure 3.1). The office newsletter is distributed worldwide over the Internet (figure 3.2). In addition, the firm created a CD to educate potential clients about the office and its areas of specialization (figure 3.3). It promotes their expertise in computer visualization and high-end 3-D architectural modeling and design through the distribution of their Virtuel Model CD (figure 3.4). The firm's minidisks and miniprint business cards are also excellent promotional materials (figure 3.5).

The personal computer, combined with relatively inexpensive peripherals such as printers, scanners, modems, CD and DVD drives, graphic tablets, digital cameras, and page-layout and illustration software, has enabled marketing professionals to create high-quality graphics that can be approved in-house and forwarded directly to printing houses for production. For example, postcards created from images on the Web site for Graham Gund Architects, in Boston, Massachusetts, are cleverly packaged in a transparent vellum envelope and used to develop awareness of their special projects, awards, staff appointments, and Web address (figures 3.6, 3.7).

3.3. Office CD for gmp.

3.4. "Virtuel Model" CD for gmp. Quantity: 15,000; cost: 8,000 euros.

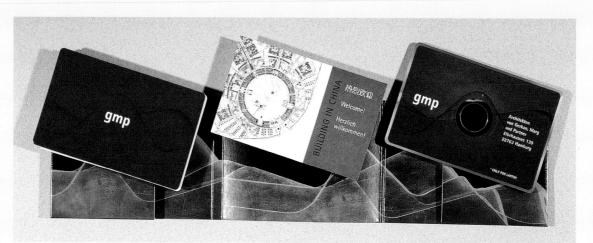

3.5. Business card CD and related miniprint materials for gmp. Quantity: 1,000; cost: 7,400 euros.

3.6. Postcard from Web site homepage for Graham Gund Architects (www.grahamgund.com).
Quantity: 2,000; cost: $1,500.

3.7. Project announcement card and Web site for
Graham Gund Architects. Cost: $7,500.

Digital technology has also made it possible to easily digitize existing photography, slides, print, and archival materials for assimilation into different media formats and digital communications. Receptive marketing instruments, such as a Web page, require viewers to seek out the page and browse at their leisure. An example is the Web site for RKW (Rhode Kellermann Wawrowsky), in Dusseldorf, Germany, featuring a portfolio of international projects that allows potential clients to review the work of this European architecture firm (figure 3.8). Assertive instruments, such as an e-mail brochure or a CD/DVD presentation, are sent to current and prospective clients for immediate viewing.

Brochures in electronic form can be used to highlight a new project or marketing campaign. They usually include specific information that works as a "teaser" to pique interest and attract a client to the firm's Web page for additional information.

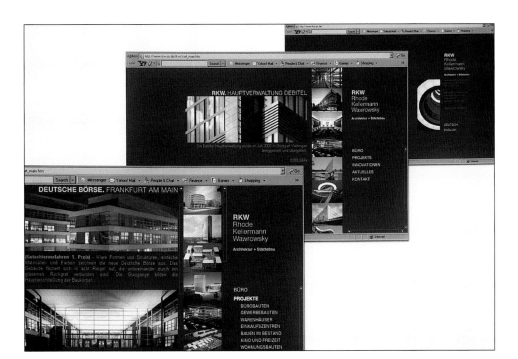

3.8. Web site featuring portfolio of projects for RKW (Rhode Kellermann Wawrowsky) (www.rkw-as.de).

3.9. Website for cepezed (www.cezeped.nl/main.html).

Cepezed, in Delft, the Netherlands, uses both their Web site (figure 3.9) and their CD (figures 3.10, 3.11) as a portfolio of architecture projects to reach their client base and show their unique array of well-designed products.

The design of both a Web site and a CD requires a clear graphic organization of projects and text with easy-to-navigate menu and details.

The Internet and Web Sites

Internet communication, such as Web sites, provides several advantages over traditional print communications. Digital technology is more economical than print and bulk mail and it allows for instant dissemination of information and access to a global audience. In addition, Web pages can be readily updated.

Most design firms' Web sites include all or some of the following:

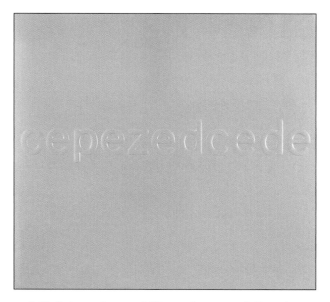

3.10. Embossed cover of CD case for cepezed. Quantity: 1,000; cost: 450 euros; 2002.

3.11. CD case and CD for cepezed.

- Home page
- Firm profile
- Solution groups (such as cities and communities, health, learning, office)
- Practices (such as interiors, preservation, lighting design)
- Current and past projects
- Media attention

The Web site of Murphy/Jahn, in Chicago, Illinois, offers a menu of items including current work, firm profile, media, and projects throughout the world (figure 3.12); the Eames Office's Web sites also has global reach (figure 3.13).

Digital formats for Internet-based communications are relatively universal and can be viewed on any computer system regardless of the operating system. The ease of access to the Web and availability of software for developing digital communications provide firms with a new media channel that can enhance communication, coordination, and collaboration with clients. The Web

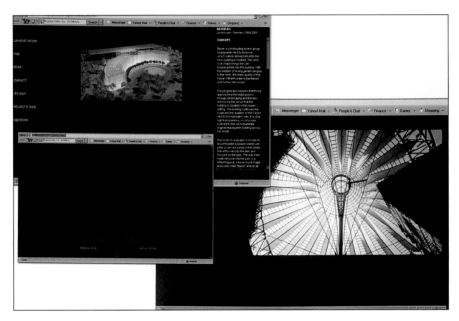

3.12. Web site for Murphy/Jahn (www.murphyjahn.com).

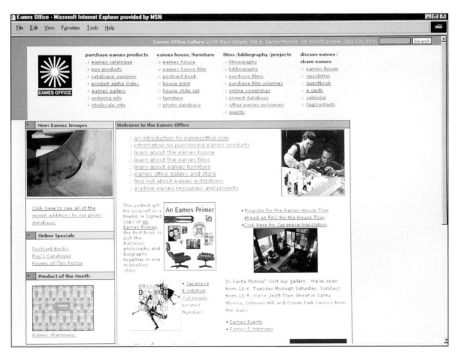

3.13. Web site for Eames Office (www.eamesoffice.com).

site for architectus™, in North Sydney, Australia, clearly describes the firm's international design experience and accomplishments (figures 3.14, 3.15). It contains a full menu, is well written and easy to navigate, and includes tools to communicate with clients on specific projects. The

Web site for Creative Logic, Inc., in Peoria, Illinois, includes a homepage, services page, company information page, and page featuring the firm's projects (figure 3.16).

Search Engines and Links

Traditional print marketing cam-

paigns are designed to identify and reach a few potential clients. The Internet works in reverse, connecting clients seeking design services with professionals who can help them. When you establish a Web domain for your firm, you must carefully identify key words that can be used

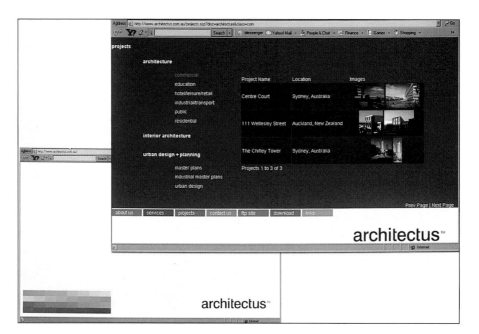

3.14. Web site for architectus™ (www.architectus.com.au).

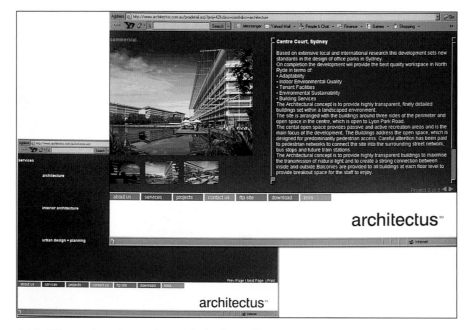

3.15. Office projects featured on Web site for architectus™.

to direct search engines like Yahoo and Google to your site. These key words can be based upon specific architectural services or special expertise. You can also take advantage of client, consultant, vendor, and organizational affiliations by having their Web sites provide links to your firm's site. The HarleyEllis Web site includes links to partner companies and information on careers and the industry (figure 3.17). Resolution: 4 Architecture in New York provides useful links to online and print journals that have written about them, making it easy for potential clients to read about their commissions and recent work (figure 3.18). The American Institute of Architects (AIA) home page is a window into networking and resources for those looking for an architect as well as those seeking information on the profession (figure 3.19). The site provides links to a national listing of architectural firms that can be viewed by service or region. For

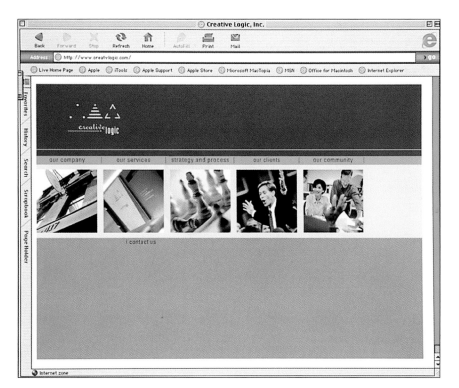

3.16. Web site for Creative Logic, Inc. (www.creativelogic.com). Cost: $40,000.

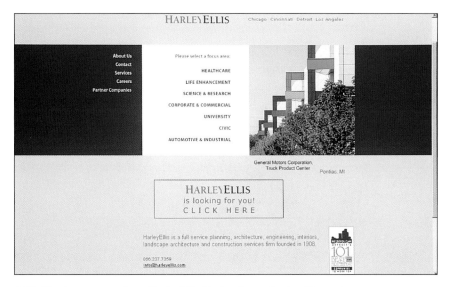

3.17. The home page from HarleyEllis Design (www.harleyellis.com).

example, the AIA has local, regional, and national membership. The Chicago Architecture Foundation's Web site offers links to the AIA and AIA Chicago branch (figure 3.20).

Film, Video, and Animation
Electronic media presentations have become independent art forms based on architecture, photography, graphic design, motion graphics, and even

cinematography. Because the content is ultimately in digital form, it can be easily updated and refreshed. Archimation®, in Berlin, Germany, is an architectural and digital media com-

3.18. Web site for Resolution: 4 Architecture (www.re4a.com).

3.19. Home page for American Institute of Architects (www.aia.org).

pany that provides visual communications for architects and developers. Their Web site showcases various design, illustration, and animation visualizations that are projects of the firm (figures 3.21–3.23).

Electronic brochures and other forms of advertisement can be customized to target a client's unique concerns. This makes the material seem particularly personalized and relevant and greatly enhances the potential for making connections and building relationships. Video can be used to show a president speaking about the firm's history and credentials or a project team leader demonstrating expertise or providing commentary concerning a project's critical issues. Videotapes from gmp demonstrate office projects and unique engineering research models (figure 3.24).

Time-based communications af-

3.20. Home page for Chicago Architecture Foundation (www.architecture.org).

3.21. "Berlin Main Station" case study page on Web site for archimation®.

3.22. "Berlin Main Station" case study page on Web site for archimation®.

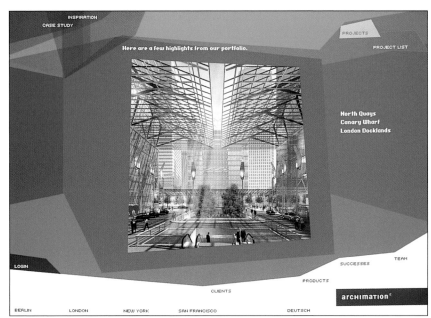

3.23. "Highlights from office portfolio" page on Web site for archimation®.

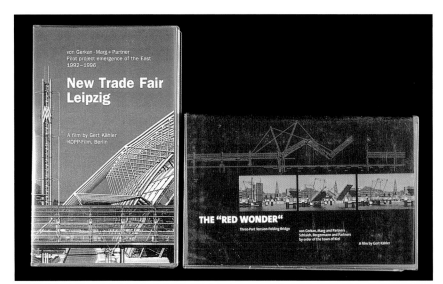

3.24. Office videotapes for gmp (von Gerkan, Marg und Partner, Architects).

ford designers the opportunity to communicate the experience of moving through an architectural space in a way that still photographs and drawings cannot. Video clips, virtual reality, and animation have opened a window to marketing the spatial experience of architectural form and materials as never before. Marketing professionals can now create presentations that take prospective clients into and through architectural interior, urban, and landscape space. The Web site of Lab architecture studio, in Melbourne, Australia, includes a provocative opening page with an animated menu, superb graphics, and a large range of project presentations (figures 3.25, 3.26).

CDs and DVDs

Multimedia productions typically combine various formats and are becoming the marketing and design

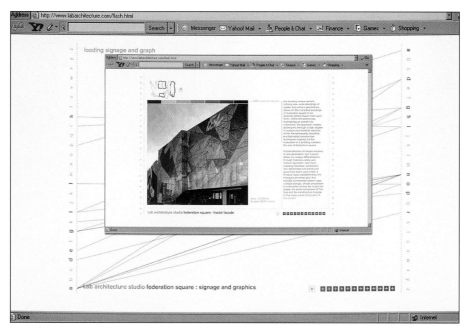

3.25. Web site for Lab architecture studio (www.labarchitecture.com). Cost: approx. Australian $10,000; 2001.

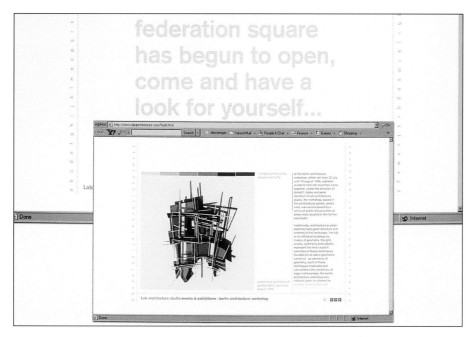

3.26. "Federation Square" page on Web site for Lab architecture studio.

media tool for the twenty-first century. CDs and DVDs are inexpensive and a single disk can house large volumes of data. Ellerbe Becket's CD, shown in figure 3.27, is one component of their office identity program, which includes brochures, postcards, flyers, and a Web site that advertise their main brand concept "Mission Critical Marketing." Bentel Abramson & Partners, in Houghton, South Africa, has designed a printed table of contents that is coordinated with the projects included on their office CD (figure 3.28). The relatively small size of a CD is convenient for mailing to clients. Making copies of a CD is inexpensive.

The minidisk is the same size as and looks like a business card but contains much more information. It

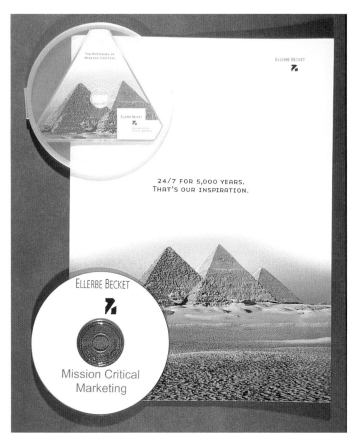

3.27. CD and brochure for Ellerbe Becket. 9 x 12 inches.

3.28. CD portfolio of significant projects with printed table of contents for Bentel Abramson & Partners. 8¼ x 11¾ inches.

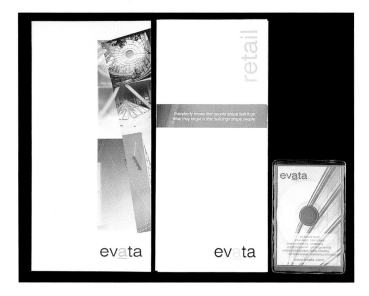

3.29. Flyers and minidisk business card for evata. 8½ x 11½ inches.
Quantity: 500 minidisks; cost: $500.

can be played in a regular CD drive and can provide a presentation for prospective clients to review at their convenience. Evata, in Helsinki, Finland, includes a minidisk with office flyers offering an overview of the firm's activities (figure 3.29).

The Digital Media Package

The most progressive marketing strategies incorporate electronic communications intended to capture the client's imagination by means of Web sites, e-mail, video, animation, virtual reality, and multimedia. All of the new digital media applications can demonstrate the experience of architecture and design through a comprehensive sensory presentation of visuals, sound, and movement. A digital media package is a powerful tool that can communicate design vision and complex problem solving clearly and in a graphic format that is easily understood by the client. Skillful and clever use of such a package can strengthen a firm's brand and image by demonstrating its technological sophistication and quality, as is the case in Sheppard Robson's bifold office brochure, bifold CD, office tear sheets, flyers, and special project brochures (figures 3.30–3.33).

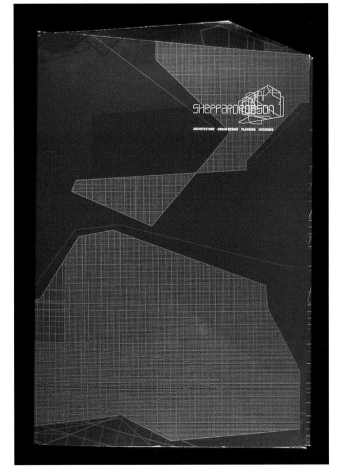

3.30. Bifold office brochure (cover) for Sheppard Robson. 8½ x 13 inches. Quantity: 1,000; cost: £5 each.

3.31. "Toyota Motor Corporation" special project brochure (cover) for Sheppard Robson. 8½ x 13 inches. Quantity: 500; cost: £10 each.

3.32. Bifold office brochure, bifold CD, office tear sheets, flyers, and special project brochure for Sheppard Robson. Quantity: 250; cost: £10 each.

3.33. "Toyota Motor Corporation" special project brochure (interior spread) for Sheppard Robson.

4. Advertising Media

The goal in any form of advertising for architects is to tell the firm's story. Advertising is written and designed specifically to focus on the accomplishments of the firm, introduce its various departments and staff, and cultivate an overall awareness of its achievements. Awards, competitions, significant commissions, and innovative projects are integral to the story of the firm. Three categories of advertising media are relevant: the professional press (architecture and design journals), the business press (business newspapers and specialized newsletters), and the public media (radio and television, newspapers and magazines, and direct mail).

Advertising addresses competition among firms on all types and sizes of projects. To develop an in-depth understanding of your clients' interests, business habits, and development practices, you must be aware of the publications and forms of advertising to which the target market—administrators, trustees, developers, facilities managers—responds. The purpose of most public-sector advertising is to create broad awareness of a company and build the consumer's desire for its products or services without the direct involvement of a salesman. In contrast, for architects and designers, the function of advertising is to support a limited but highly focused direct sales effort with

limited media advertising and other materials.

Media Ads

Specialized business practice journals produced by the Standard Rate and Data Services (SRDS), such as *Business Publication Rates and Data Book*, quote the costs for ads in relation to various determinants of size, complexity of graphic image, color, frequency of reproduction, and regional or national editions. These guides include a summary of the readership, closing dates for reserving space, and the representative's contact information.

Exploring the available source materials for the cost of advertising leads to an informed understanding of expense to suit an office promotion budget. It also facilitates a decision-making process that is based on an understanding of priorities, expense, and risk. You should take time to explore your firm's potential for supplementing traditional marketing methods and coordinating with other promotion campaigns.

Public Relations Kits and the Press

Public relations kits of strategic information regarding the firm's background, accomplishments, staff, and areas of specialization are excellent tools for architecture and design firms. These kits can be offered at

conferences, open-house presentations, and media interviews. The format varies from firm to firm, but commonly comprises a bifolder containing identity pieces, articles, newsletters, flyers, and small brochures that focus on telling the story of the firm. Public relations kits work best when they are accompanied by a letter of introduction addressed to a specific individual. The strategy is to introduce the firm in a personable way and focus on a recent project, competition, award, or other news, such as a successful new partnership between offices.

Biltmore, a building and development firm in Troy, Michigan, has refined the art of a bifold brochure public relations kit into an attention-grabbing, hand-illustrated marketing instrument that people want to pick up and read (figure 4.1). The contents are savvy, containing plentiful visual information about properties and plans, a new development project, and the firm's biography and staff resumes, all focusing on the firm's reputation as a preeminent builder/developer in the Detroit metropolitan community.

The bifolder public relations kit for Loebl Schlossman & Hackl concentrates on office performance and top projects (figure 4.2). The kit contains an office brochure, business card, and tear sheets that broadly introduce the firm's goals, areas of specialization, and recent projects of note.

Public relations kits do not necessarily focus solely on the firm and its accomplishments. Karlsberger, in Columbus, Ohio, created a twist on the public relations kit concept by including a strong representation of the firm's brand slogan (figures 4.3, 4.4). Their "Questions, Choices, Solutions" postcards make a strong first impression while simultaneously introducing the other materials in the kit.

Obviously, visual representation is vital to creating an instantaneous impression of quality design, identity,

4.1. Bifold brochure public relations kit for Biltmore. 9 x 12 inches.
Quantity: 1,500; cost: $5 per unit (made to order).

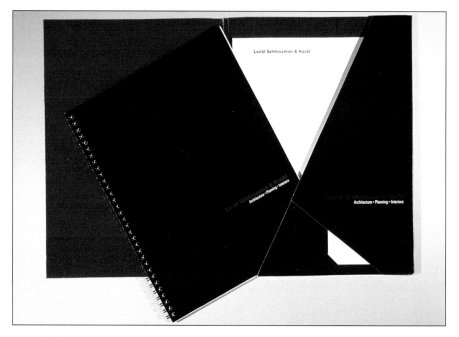

4.2. Bifolder with office brochure, business card, and tear sheets for Loebl Schlossman & Hackl. 12 x 9 inches. Quantity: 700; cost: $8.13 per unit.

4.3. Bifolder (cover) for Karlsberger. 12 x 9 inches.

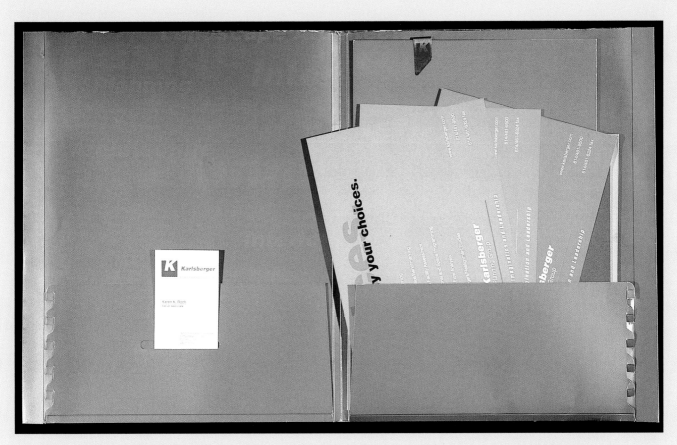

4.4. Bifolder press kit containing "Questions, Choices, Solutions" postcards and background materials for Karlsberger.

and performance. The press kit for Cambridge Seven Associates, Inc., in Cambridge, Massachusetts, makes a very strong color statement in vibrant red and blue, underscoring the firm's confidence while immediately draw-ing the viewer's attention to its contents (figures 4.5, 4.6). Identity elements, the firm overview, and special areas of emphasis accompany trifold brochures about the firm.

Magazines and Newspapers

Successful advertising comes from an intelligent blend of graphics, writing, motivational research, business acumen, and great timing. Architecture and design are highly competitive

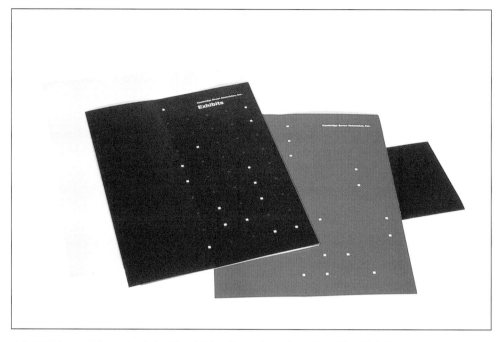

4.5. Bifolder and its contents for Cambridge Seven Associates, Inc. 8½ x 11 inches. Quantity: 2,000 of each brochure; cost: $7,440; 2002.

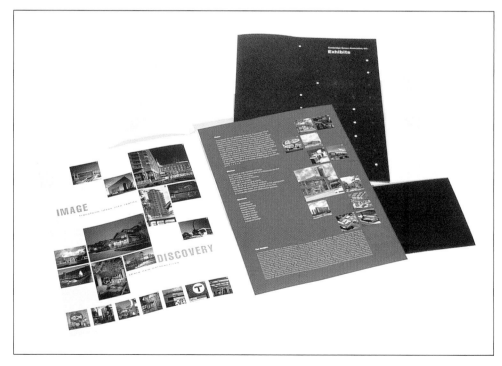

4.6. Bifolder and its contents for Cambridge Seven Associates, Inc.

businesses that require diligent research and understanding before making a costly investment in top magazines and journals.

The ideal in marketing, of course, is to have someone else tell your story for you. Therein lies one of the savviest approaches to advertising: to secure media and press stories about your firm that include client testimonials. Requesting reprints of these interviews, articles, or cover features makes for excellent public relations and advertising for the firm. Reprints of feature articles should be included in your public relations kit or used separately as mailers to significant clients and future prospects. Resolution: 4 Architecture, in New York City, uses a reprint from *Interior Design* magazine, which featured the "light box" design for a client's living loft in Tribeca, New York (figure 4.7). A reprint from *Interiors* magazine showcases the McCann-Erickson Worldwide 16th Floor Renovation, also by Resolution: 4 Architecture (figure 4.8).

Although the cost of advertising space in such top publications as the *Wall Street Journal*, *Forbes Magazine*, and *Business Weekly* is out of reach for smaller firms, ads can be purchased in local newspapers, magazines, and general business journals by practitioners with smaller budgets.

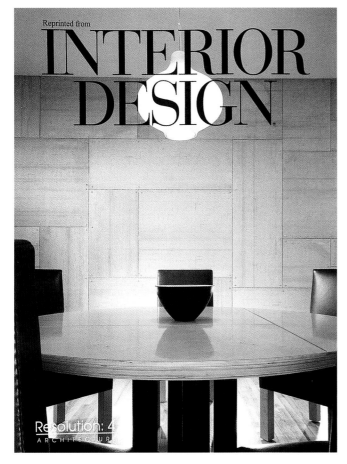

4.7. Reprint from *Interior Design* magazine, September 1997, for Resolution: 4 Architecture. Photography by Paul Warchol. 11 x 8½ inches. Quantity: varies; cost: approx. $1 per unit.

4.8. Reprint from *Interiors* magazine, January 1999, for Resolution: 4 Architecture. Photography by Eduard Hueber/Arch Photo. 11 x 8½ inches.

A modest announcement of a recent award, competition, or successful project completion, along with the name of the firm or firms and their locations, is a typical format for large and small firm advertisements. The well-designed Web site of the Smith-Group, headquartered in Detroit, Michigan, incorporates a "News & Media" page that is intended to keep the public and news media informed of the firm's activities and projects (figure 4.9). Categories include News Releases, Media Kit, Media Sources, and 150 Years of SmithGroup. The News Releases section offers brief descriptions of office projects highlighted for the press; the Media Kit

4.9. "News & Media" page on Web site for the SmithGroup (www.smith-group.com/aboutus/newsmedia.asp). Cost: no charge (produced in-house).

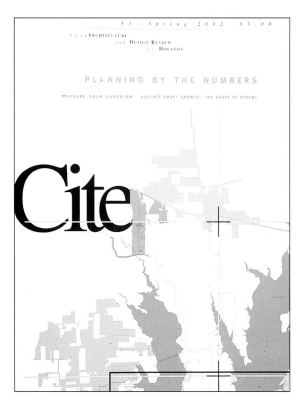

4.10. *Cite: The Architecture and Design Review of Houston*, spring edition, 2002. 10¾ x 14 inches. Quantity: 5,000; cost: $20,000; 2002.

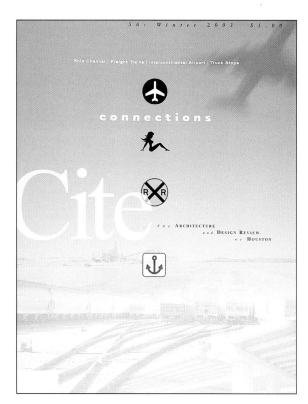

4.11. *Cite: The Architecture and Design Review of Houston*, winter edition. Quantity: 5,000; cost: $20,000; 2003.

summarizes important facts about the architecture firm and its focus in design; Media Sources includes the background education and experience of the SmithGroup staff who are experts in various sectors of the firm's practice, such as medical, education, and government; and 150 Years of SmithGroup provides an in-depth history of the firm.

In addition to purchased advertising space in newspapers and magazines, reviews that appear in the design section of significant newspapers, written by architecture critics, are an ideal advertising and promotion vehicle. An unsolicited review can establish an office's reputation among the leading practitioners in their area of specialization.

Architectural Journals

Architects and marketing directors take special pains to send summary descriptions with visuals of recent accomplishments to prominent architectural journals in the hope of having a story written on the subject of the firm's work. A well-written article in a professional journal is usually more effective than any number of ads a potential client may—or may not—see.

Cite: The Architecture and Design Review of Houston, a publication of the Rice Design Alliance at Rice University, designed by the Minor Design Group in Houston, Texas, is a large-format urban planning and architecture journal with a flourishing national readership (figures 4.10, 4.11). The publication presents articles and reviews of noteworthy architecture and planning projects, competitions, and proposals, which fosters broad public awareness, discussion, and debate.

World Architecture magazine focuses attention on architecture across five continents (figure 4.12). The March 2001 edition, titled "Northern

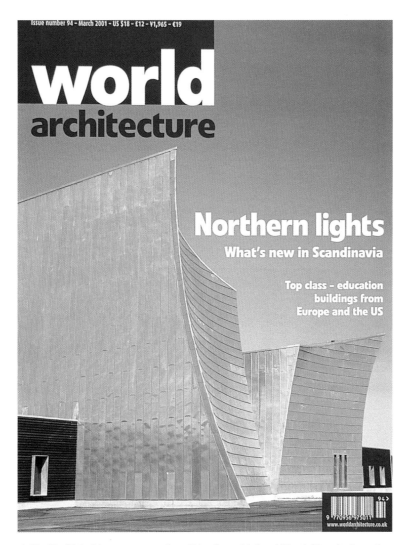

4.12. *World Architecture* magazine, "Northern Lights: What's New in Scandinavia," March 2001.

Lights: What's New in Scandinavia," featured Nordic architectural design projects and Scandinavian design directions. The international design press offers architects opportunities to be seen internationally. A reprint from *The Architectural Review* magazine titled "Copenhagen Culture" includes a feature story on the work of Soren Robert Lund Architects, in Copenhagen, Denmark (figure 4.13).

Some firms create their own annual reports, special editions, and journals annually or semiannually to supplement outside reviews. The *ARUP Annual Report* (figure 4.14) and *The ARUP Millennium Journal* (figure 4.15) exemplify the London-based

4.13. Reprint from *The Architectural Review* magazine, "Copenhagen Culture," including feature story on Soren Robert Lund Architects. 7 x 11½ inches.

firm's project range, activities, and accomplishments. As the field of facilities management flourished throughout the 1990s and into the new millennium, firms that specialize in this area of architecture and devel- opment have made headway by pub- lishing their expertise. Global, a con- sulting company in Brussels, Bel- gium, specializes in design, project, and facility management and pub- lishes annual editions on facilities management for development firms, building construction companies, architecture firms, and the general professional audience (figures 4.16– 4.18).

Resolution: 4 Architecture pub-

4.14. *ARUP Annual Report*, 2001, for ARUP Architects. 8¼ x 11¾ inches. Quantity: 12,500; cost: $40,000; annual.

4.15. *The ARUP Millennium Journal*, 2/2001, for ARUP Archi- tects. 8¼ x 11¾ inches. Quantity: 11,000; cost: $40,000 ($3.64 per unit); 2002.

4.16. 2002 brochure (cover)
for Global. 9 x 11¼ inches.

4.17. 2002 brochure (interior
spread) for Global.

4.18. Interior design project
featured in 2002 brochure
for Global.

lishes large-format paperbacks that feature special projects and are aimed at an urban planning and architecture audience interested in the design excellence of the firm and noteworthy planning projects (figures 4.19, 4.20). The publications include a statement of the firm's philosophy, partners' biographies, and invited essays.

The 1995–2000 portfolio brochure of Jones Coulter Young Architects and Urban Designers, in Perth, Western Australia, states the firm's philosophy and accomplishments and includes a vivid photographic essay of completed projects (figure 4.21). These photographic essays attract attention while serving as mini-portfolio office promotions.

Murphy/Jahn, in Chicago, Illinois,

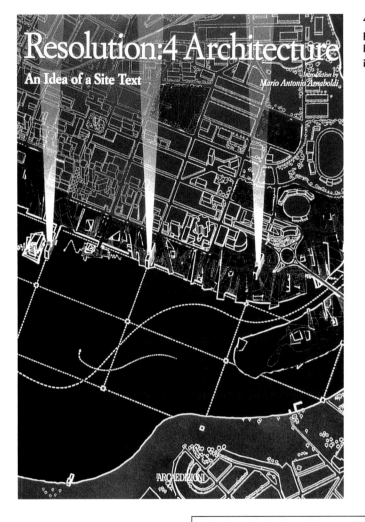

4.19. "An Idea of a Site Text," large-format paperback for Resolution: 4 Architecture. Published by l'Arcaedizioni, Milan, Italy. 13½ x 9½ inches. Quantity: 6,000; cost: $25,000.

4.20. "An Idea of a Site Text" (interior spread) for Resolution: 4 Architecture.

produces specific journals devoted to special design sectors of the firm such as high-rise design (figure 4.22).

Specialty magazines devoted to architecture, landscape architecture, interior design, urban planning, and environmental design are abundant and vary in scope from regional to international publications. They are sometimes self-published but more frequently are published by various commercial publishers with an archi-

4.21. 1995–2000 portfolio brochure (center spreads) for Jones Coulter Young Architects and Urban Designers. 9½ x 12¼ inches.

4.22. Office brochure on high-rise design for Murphy/Jahn. 10 x 10 inches.

tectural focus. *A+U* (architecture and urbanism), an international publication that devotes attention to major design projects in urban centers, produces special issues focused on the work of individual firms of great reputation and critical acknowledgment. In recent years, Helmut Jahn of Murphy/Jahn has been the recipient of several feature articles and special editions in the magazine (figures 4.23, 4.24).

4.23. *A+U* magazine (special edition), "Helmut Jahn Hotel Kempinski, Munich Airport." 9 x 12 inches.

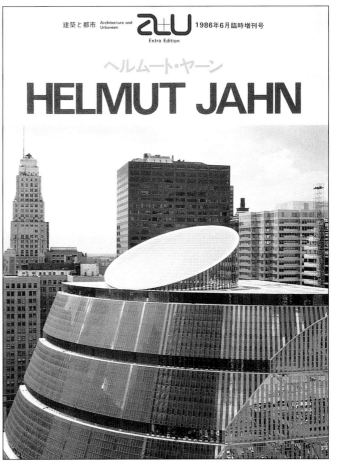

4.24. *A+U* magazine (special edition), "Helmut Jahn." 9 x 12 inches.

5. Materials for Seminars, Lectures, Interviews, Trade Shows, Conferences, and Conventions

Presentations at seminars, lectures, interviews, trade shows, conferences, and conventions are an important ingredient in meeting and attracting potential clients. The firm that is rewarded with a commission is often the firm that has built a competitive edge through presentation strategies that include a face-to-face discussion of designs, budgets, and qualifications. Marketing materials play the dual role of educating the client during and after the one-on-one meeting. Clients make critical decisions based on ideas brought to the table in person as well as through published literature that illustrates the content, commitment, capability, and credentials of the design team to find good solutions to problems in an efficient, economic, and pleasing way.

Plan information with an understanding of what will be remembered. It is better for a client or review committee to reference details and long lists of facts after the one-on-one meeting has occurred. Technical information in reports and handouts can be reviewed later by a committee or interview team. Successful presentations (in person, print, and digital forms) for meetings of almost every type begin with the unique characteristics of the proposal emphasized at the outset and

at the closing of the presentation. An articulate presentation and summary of design content to a prospective client is evidence of the capability of managing the project from conception through construction and suggests that the size, complexity, and design challenges of the job are within the experience and expertise of your firm. A history of similar projects may work well to support these points and help persuade clients to select your firm.

Seminars, Lectures, and Interviews

Specialists in every aspect of architecture and design often make lecture presentations to groups to demonstrate their unique abilities and services. Speaking about the firm and answering questions on a one-on-one basis or with small groups works best when you have supplemental materials such as attractive media kits, tear sheets, brochures, and portfolios. Know the venue before you begin planning your presentation; conference halls, for example, are neither conducive to nor equipped for auditorium-style presentations. One of the key ingredients in planning presentations for seminars, lectures, and interviews is leaving plenty of time following a presentation to meet the audience, which may include a future client. It

is advantageous to follow up a seminar or lecture with a presentation of office literature and a post-session survey in which attendees are asked to evaluate the presentation. More information, such as the names of potential clients to add to a firm's database and mailing list, can be gained or provided through follow-up communication. Informational sessions, whether in person or through the Internet or regular mail, can lead to a fruitful exchange and new contacts. You can also increase attendance at seminars and lectures by sending out invitations to community groups, civic clubs, business associations, and leaders of financial and cultural institutions.

Interviews held at conferences or in an office environment call for print materials, models, presentation boards, and a laptop computer to illustrate and support important concepts. Print materials are always appropriate in interviews and presentations to small groups or single individuals. Many architecture firms rely on print materials and Powerpoint presentations for seminars, lectures, and interviews to represent the firm's history and expertise: an example is HarleyEllis, in Southfield, Michigan (figures 5.1–5.3). Their Powerpoint presentations have strong contrasts in color and typography and are

Our Background

- Founded in 1908
- 300 Person Full-Service Firm

5.1. PowerPoint presentation page featuring firm background and history for HarleyEllis.

Automotive & Industrial

- Ameritech
- Detroit Edison
- Ford Motor Company
- Chrysler Corporation
- General Motors Corporation
- Hawtal Whiting
- Hines
- ITT Automotive

Ford Fairlane Training and Development Center

General Motors Truck Product Center

HARLEYELLIS

5.2. PowerPoint presentation page featuring list of credentials of university buildings for HarleyEllis.

University

- Central Michigan University
- Indiana University
- Interlochen Center for the Arts
- Kettering University
- Michigan State University
- Oakland University
- Saginaw Valley State University
- University of Detroit Mercy
- Wayne State University
- Western Michigan University
- University of Detroit Mercy

Central Michigan University Music Building

*Saginaw Valley State University
Business and Professional Development Center*

HARLEYELLIS

5.3. PowerPoint presentation page featuring list of credentials of automotive and industrial buildings for HarleyEllis.

designed to be viewed across the distance of a conference room or from the close proximity of a laptop computer screen (figures 5.4–5.6). The presentations are organized with bullet points and animated with color photography, illustrations, and graphics to communicate the firm's background.

PSA (Phillips Swager Associates), in Peoria, Illinois, uses two forms of visual presentation documents during interviews for qualifications. The 11- x 17-inch presentation booklet shown in figures 5.7–5.11 is used for

5.4. PowerPoint presentation page for HarleyEllis.

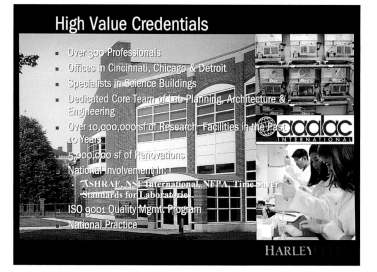

5.5. PowerPoint presentation page featuring the University of Cincinnati's Medical Sciences Building for HarleyEllis.

5.6. PowerPoint presentation page featuring Michigan State University's National Toxicology Building for HarleyEllis.

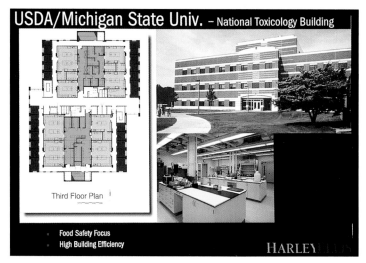

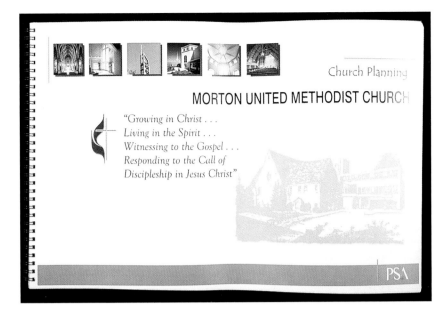

5.7. Presentation booklet (cover) for PSA (Phillips Swager Associates). 11 x 17 inches. Quantity: made to order per client; cost: $50 per unit.

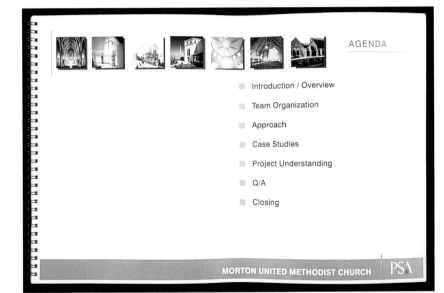

5.8. Presentation booklet (agenda) for PSA.

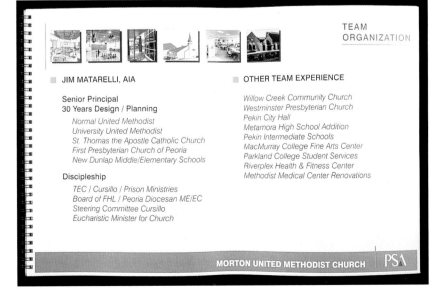

5.9. Presentation booklet (team organization) for PSA.

smaller groups of people around an office conference table. The booklet's visuals, text, charts, and graphics convey the firm's overall professional accomplishments and foster an in-depth understanding of specific design problems that correspond to the client's needs. For larger gatherings of ten or more clients in seminar rooms where information is viewed from a distance, the firm's team uses presentation boards set on easels (figures 5.12–5.14). The visuals are created with large-format color printers and mounted on gator board or foam core for easy transportation and presentation.

Trade Shows, Conferences, and Conventions

Marketing instruments at events such as trade shows are intended to attract viewers to an exhibition booth where they can see a presentation. To stand out in the crowd requires creative forms of visual communications—if only to hold the attention of the visitor long enough to communicate a message about the firm.

Brochures, articles, pamphlets, and portfolios are vital to engage visitors' interest in a firm and secure the

5.9. Presentation book-let (team organization) for PSA.

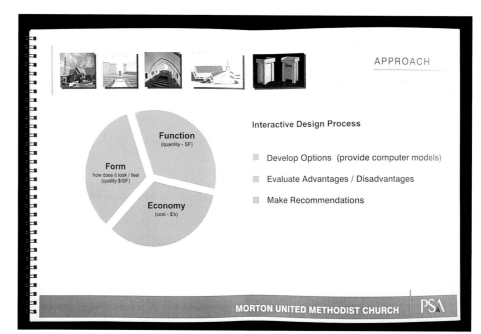

5.11. Presentation booklet (First Presbyterian Church) for PSA.

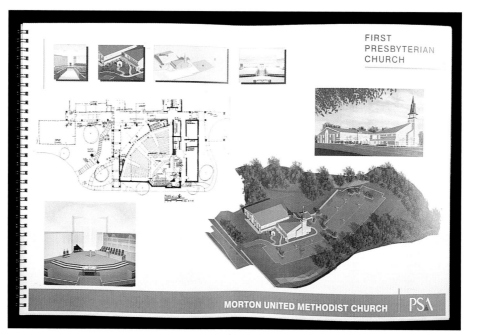

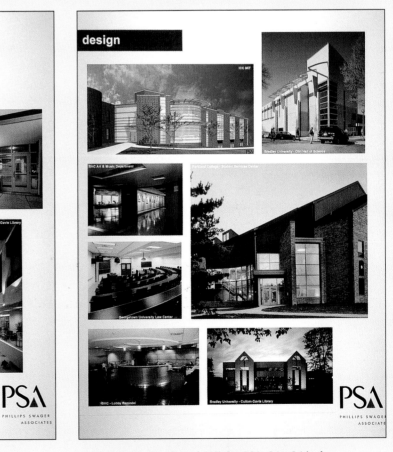

team attributes

related experience
Black Hawk College - both campuses
Community Colleges throughout Illinois

ability / capacity to perform
Largest Illinois A/E practice outside of Chicago
Established and Committed Team for Black Hawk College
Closest to Kewanee and Moline of Firm's Being Considered

in-depth understanding of requirements, expectations and environment
Conducted Studies, RAMP Applications, HP&LS Surveys
Design Recognition
Knowledge of Communities
Established Relationships with Local Contractors

service delivery
Comprehensive In-house Services
Single Point of Responsibility and Accountability

management approach
Collaborative, Interactive and Predictable

consultants
Only as needed

schedules
Knowledge of Prospective Projects / Urgency

PSA
PHILLIPS SWAGER
ASSOCIATES

5.12. Presentation board (team attributes) for PSA. 24 x 36 inches. Quantity: made to order per client; cost: $100 per unit.

5.13. Presentation board (#1) for PSA. 24 x 36 inches.

5.14. Presentation board (#2) for PSA. 24 x 36 inches.

75

firm's professional reputation. Olin Partnership's boxed portfolio booklet, shown in figure 5.15, introduces the firm in an attractive and memorable graphic representation that celebrates twenty-five years of landscape architecture and urban design achievements, collaborations, innovations, and excellence. The Olin Partnership has also produced a spirited brochure of landscape and urban design projects with clever photomontage, layered typography, and vivid color to reinforce their slogan, "Powerful Concepts, Elegant Solutions, Beautifully Made" (figures 5.16, 5.17).

A series of cleverly designed marketing instruments allows visitors to experience a firm in a number of different ways. Print materials prepared for conferences can be used for direct mail as well. The office brochure of TVS (Thompson, Ventulett, Stainback & Associates), in Atlanta, Georgia, is an elegant and striking portfolio presentation (figures 5.18–5.20). Its vellum cover builds anticipation of the full-page photographs that can be seen through it. The TVS four-panel "Interiors" brochure showcases that department of the firm; the generous

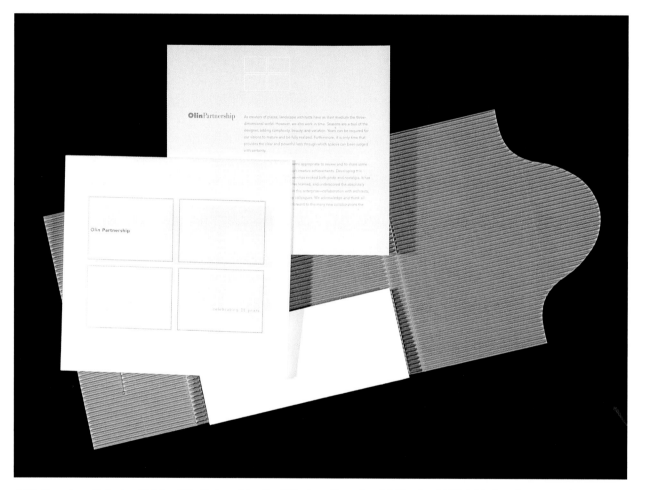

5.15. Boxed portfolio booklet for Olin Partnership. 7 x 7½ inches. Quantity: 5,000, plus 2,500 folded mailers; cost: $75,000.

5.16. Brochure for Olin Partnership. 7½ x 10¾ inches. Quantity: 7,500, plus 5,000 mailers; cost: $25,000.

5.17. Brochure for Olin Partnership.

5.18. Office brochure for TVS (Thompson, Ventulett, Stainback & Associates). 8½ x 11 inches.

5.19. Office brochure (interior spread with full-page photographs) for TVS.

5.20. Office brochure (interior spread with full-page photographs) for TVS.

use of white space on the page acts as a mat for the photographs (figures 5.21, 5.22).

Nothing succeeds like success. A handout such as the AIA Architecture Firm Award 2000 announcement traces the history of design awards garnered by TVS and offers talking points at conferences and meetings (figures 5.23, 5.24).

Concepts That Work

Branding plays an important role in catching the interest of visitors and should offer an idea, slogan, or carefully crafted phrase that summarizes

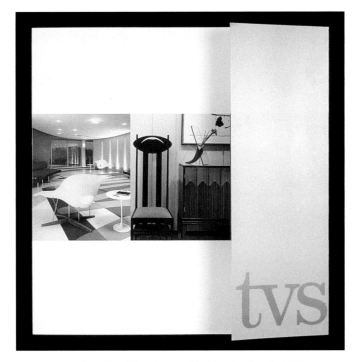

5.21. "Interiors" brochure with identity flap for TVS. 8½ x 8½ inches.

5.22. "Interiors" brochure with foldout panels for TVS.

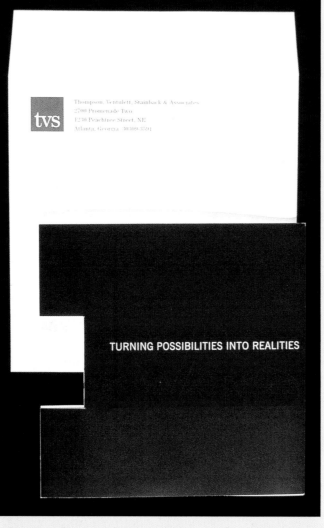

**5.23. "AIA Architecture Firm Award 2000" pop-up mailer for TVS.
6 x 6 inches.**

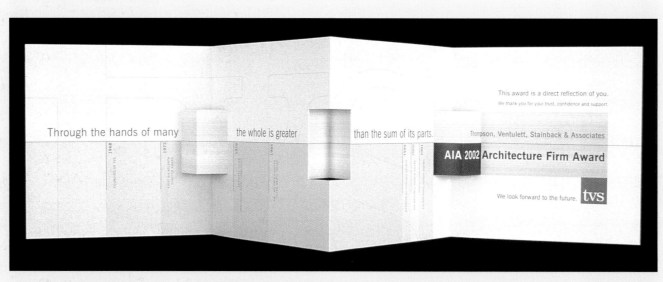

5.24. "AIA Architecture Firm Award 2000" pop-up mailer (open) for TVS.

the special attributes and personality of a firm. The brochure for Karlsberger, in Columbus, Ohio, develops the branding concept "Questions, Choices, Solutions," gives background information about the firm's design philosophy, and makes it easy for the viewer to open an introductory dialogue with the firm (figures 5.25, 5.26). An elaborate print presentation will not be successful if the firm's identity is not prominent in the piece and on its cover. Chetwood associates, in London, England, creates branding in its large-format brochures with strong visuals and slogans such as "Pushing Ideas" reflecting the firm's aggressive position, energy, and enthusiasm for high-quality design (figures 5.27– 5.29). The corporate journal is filled with high-quality photographs and spirited typographic message overlays—for example, "We value team-

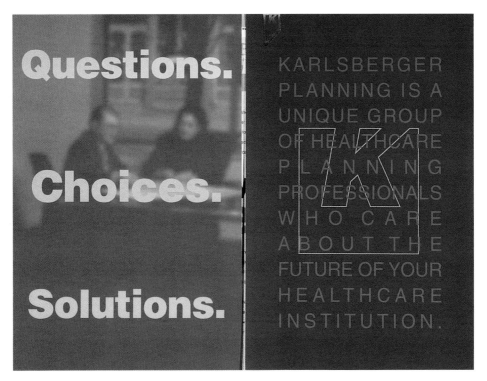

5.25. "Questions, Choices, Solutions" brochure for Karlsberger. 10 x 13 inches.

5.26. "Questions, Choices, Solutions" brochure (interior) for Karlsberger.

work"—to engage the reader. The SmithGroup JJR's office brochures reinforce their overall mission "to create a true sense of place": flyers from various departments are designed to coordinate with the CD and focus on areas of specialization within the firm (figure 5.30). The four-panel brochure with announcement mailer, and all of the firm's literature, are coordinated in a well-designed graphic presentation (figure 5.31). Special project brochures are developed to showcase projects about "cities and communities" and "water-

5.27. "Pushing Ideas" brochure for Chetwood associates. 9 x 12 inches. Quantity: 600 published since 2001; cost: £8 per brochure; 2001.

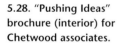

5.28. "Pushing Ideas" brochure (interior) for Chetwood associates.

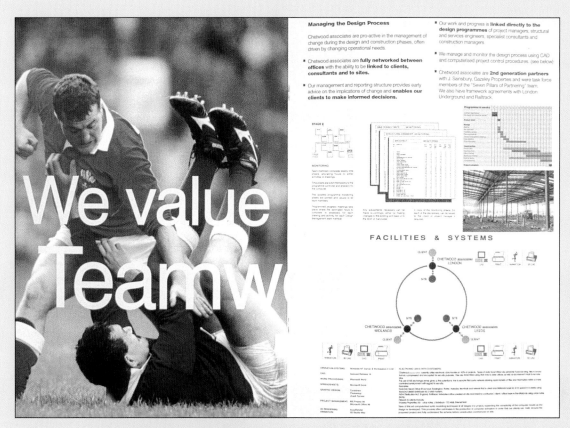

5.29. "Pushing Ideas" brochure (interior) for Chetwood associates.

5.30. Flyers for SmithGroup JJR. 3¾ x 8½ inches. Quantity: 2,000; cost: $11,000; 2001

fronts" and present the range of the practice in planning and landscape architecture (figure 5.32).

The most effective way to introduce a firm to the public at conferences, conventions, and public presentations is a print piece that demonstrates the range of work of the office. This may be a mini-portfolio that entices the visitor to arrange a meeting where a larger and more impressive print or digital presentation can be offered. The "2002 Portfolio" brochure created by Soren Robert Lund Architects features commissions from 1996–2002, competitions, exhibitions, affiliations, prizes, and publications (figure 5.33). The presentation is clean and concise, with brief introductions to the categories of their work over the pre-

5.31. Four-panel brochure with announcement mailer and firm literature for SmithGroup JJR. 8½ x 11 inches. Quantity: 1,500; cost: $4,000; 2001.

5.32. "Cities and communities" and "waterfronts" brochures for SmithGroup JJR. 8½ x 11 inches. Quantity: 1,500 each; cost: $3,000 each; 2000–2002.

vious six years of their practice. When a design firm is highly specialized, the brochure content must go directly to the heart of the firm and its work. Creative Logic, Inc., in Peoria, Illinois, created its "Design That Works" illustrated brochure to showcase the environment for office furniture and design services offered by Lincoln Office Company (figure 5.34). Attractive, vivid graphic design captures the curiosity of the viewer and presents the firm as a provider of contemporary office furniture and design services.

5.33. "2002 Portfolio" brochure for Soren Robert Lund Architects. 7 x 11½ inches. Quantity: 50–70 per year; cost: $33 per copy ($1,980 in 2002: 60 studio folders given out); start-up production cost: $3,000.

5.34. "Design That Works," illustrated brochure for Lincoln Office designed by Creative Logic, Inc. 6 x 10 inches. Quantity: 3,500; cost of printing: approx. $6,500.

6. Special Events and Unique Approaches

Occasionally special events invite new and unique approaches to marketing communications. The venues for these marketing materials include open houses, cultural and sporting events, and exhibitions, as well as conventions, and seminars where the opportunity to showcase innovative forms of visual communication to a receptive audience is appropriate. Many firms take special pride in creating direct mail pieces in the form of postcards and invitations to holiday parties, concerts, and cultural events.

Announcements and Invitations

Architecture firms sometimes sponsor sporting and cultural entertainment events to cultivate clients and build relationships. Invitations should include the title of the event and the name of the sponsoring firm. Staff members who attend the events represent the office in a social setting to those who have interest in their services and expertise. Clients want to pursue a design firm that fits their own profile of needs and is knowledgeable and professional in every aspect of architectural practice.

Typically, holidays are a time for firms to deliver a personal message

6.1. Holiday cards, invitations to events, firm announcements, CD, and flyers for Nightingale Associates.

to clients and contacts. These are excellent opportunities to increase the range of a firm's activities and simultaneously promote business relationships with clients and enhance the image of the firm. Holiday greetings allow for much imagination: this is the place for two- and three-dimensional folding pieces, humor, and other creative forms to express the company's ideals and philosophy. Nightingale Associates, in Oxford, England, reinforces its branding program with multiple materials, including holiday cards,

invitations to the symphony and other cultural events, and announcements of design projects and awards, all of which incorporate the firm's signature range of blue-gray hues (figure 6.1).

Tenazas Design, in San Francisco, California, used a collage format with varied compositions of type, photography, and graphics for a series of individual announcement cards for each speaker event at the San Francisco Museum of Modern Art's Architecture Lecture Series (figure 6.2). The Minor Design Group, in

Houston, Texas, designed a series of announcement cards with collage images of text and photography for the Rice Design Alliance tours and special events sponsored by Rice University (figure 6.3).

Award announcement cards are often eye-catching, elegant designs with a more formal presentation and reserved typography and graphics. Figure 6.4 shows an Andersson-Wise Architects' concertina announcement that folds accordion-style into a self-mailer and announces their award-winning Garriott Carriage

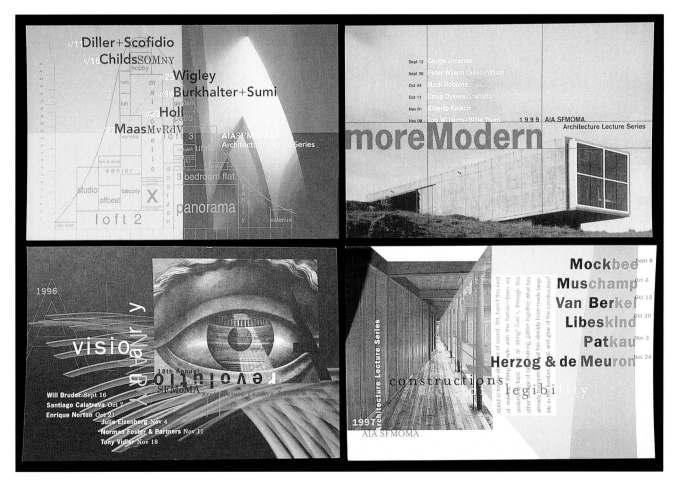

6.2. Architecture lecture series postcards by Tenazas Design. 6 x 9 inches.

6.3. Rice Design Alliance event postcards for Rice University by Minor Design Group. 6 x 8½ inches. Quantity: 5,000; cost: $1,200; 2000–2003.

6.4. Garriott Carriage House 2001 Honor Award concertina announcement for Andersson-Wise Architects. 3 x 5 inches. Quantity: 500; cost: $1,000; 2001.

House. Fanning/Howey Associates, Inc., in Celina, Ohio, produced "40 Year Celebration" bifold postcards focused on the firm's identity in the community and the firm's history of accomplishments to attract new clients (figures 6.5 and 6.6). HarleyEllis created the attractive "Reflections 2000" CD with trifold cover around the people, customers, work, and success of the firm, including award-winning design projects for the year (figures 6.7, 6.8). The firm celebrated being named AIA Michigan's "Firm of the Year" by creating a thank-you card to the staff and allied firms that contributed to achieving the award (figure 6.9). Snapshots of winning

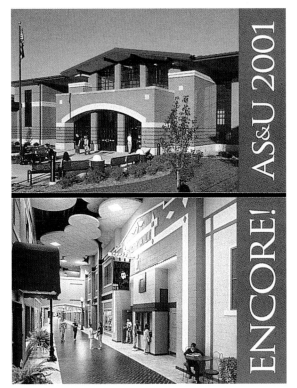

6.5. "40 Year Celebration" bifold postcards for Fanning / Howey Associates, Inc. 5¾ x 9 inches. Quantity: 2,500; cost: $6,630; 2001.

6.6. "40 Year Celebration" bifold postcards (unfolded) for Fanning / Howey Associates, Inc.

projects fill this square card, which is presented in a handsome glassine envelope. HarleyEllis also created specialty cards for new office location announcements and open house events (figure 6.10).

Posters and Calendars

Many events can serve as an impetus for an architecture firm to create a poster: a new office or location, a company anniversary, a special occasion, the completion or opening of an important project, a gallery exhibition. Posters can be commercial and economical works of art. A promotional poster can comprise materials that have already been used, such as advertisements and other print pieces, or it may be designed from scratch. The design should facilitate framing: a border can help accommodate the matting, mounting, and framing process. Herbert Lewis Kruse Blunck Architecture, in Des Moines, Iowa, used an image of a straightjacket for its

6.7. "Reflections 2000" CD (cover) for HarleyEllis. 5 x 5 inches. Quantity: 1,000; cost: $4,500; 2001.

REFLECTIONS 2000

HARLEYELLIS

6.8. "Reflections 2000" CD and trifold concertina for HarleyEllis. 5 x 5 inches.

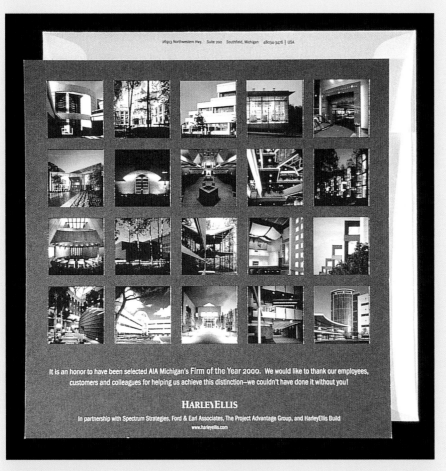

6.9. "Firm of the Year" thank-you card for HarleyEllis. 8½ x 8½ inches. Quantity: 3,500; cost: $3,465; 2000.

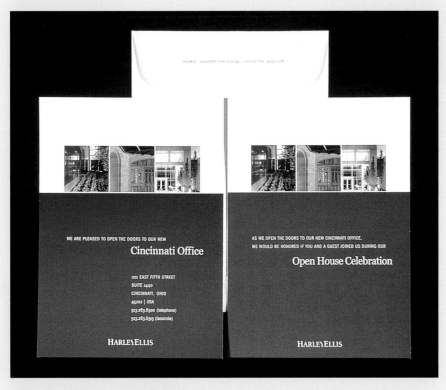

6.10. New office announcement and open-house cards for HarleyEllis. 4 x 7½ inches. Quantity: 5,000; cost: $2,500; 2001.

clever "No Jacket Required" poster advertisement, which attracts prospective employees by presenting the firm as a friendly, congenial workplace environment with a staff that has a good sense of humor (figure 6.11).

Posters do not have to be full-size movie poster–type tableaus to communicate effectively. Mini-sized posters rolled into a small mailing tube to avoid folding can be used as direct mail pieces, and they can be hung on a client's bulletin board or nearby pinup space. Careful consideration of color (or black-and-white) photography and illustrations is vital. Text should be limited to basic information such as the name of the firm and its location, along with the appropriate credit lines for photographer, artist, and graphic designer as well as copyright notice if appropriate.

Lehrer Architects, in Los Angeles,

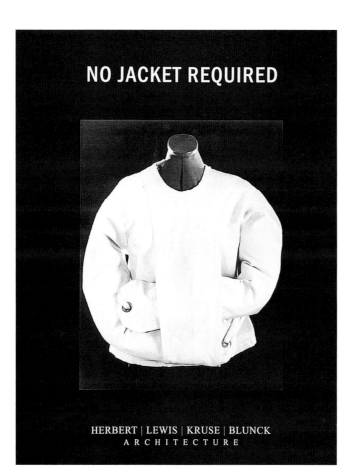

6.11. Poster advertisement for Herbert Lewis Kruse Blunck Architecture. 8½ x 11 inches. Quantity: made to order; cost: $2 per unit.

6.12. Folded postcard for Lehrer Architects. 4 x 16½ inches. Quantity: 60; cost: $3 per unit.

California, created a long folded post-card as a small poster to create awareness of the firm (figure 6.12). The SmithGroup JJR took the opposite approach with their five-foot-long landscape-format poster banner, which announces their internship program for aspiring landscape architects and planners and is most often displayed on available wall space in colleges and universities. It can be rolled and mailed in a tube (figures 6.13, 6.14).

Nightingale Associates and the SmithGroup produce calendars as awareness-building marketing instruments to send clients (figures 6.15, 6.16). The size of a CD or Zip disk jewel case, it contains separate cards for each month of the year. Music CDs were the original inspira-

6.13. Large-format internship program poster for SmithGroup JJR. 12 x 60 inches. Quantity: 500; cost: $700; 2000.

6.14. Large-format internship program poster (unfolded) for SmithGroup JJR.

tion for the jewel-case calendar concept, which has become popular as holiday gifts and mailers. HarleyEllis used a traditional layout design for their calendar, with a full-color image and the twelve months of the year printed on an 11- x 17-inch sheet (figure 6.17).

Specialty Brochures

Large and small architectural offices have opportunities throughout the year to highlight award-winning projects and competitions through print, digital, and press coverage. The typical approach is to capture a project for the office records and portfolio by producing a special print piece in celebration of a great design accomplishment. This may take various forms, but the full-color brochure is most common. Using office printers, medium-sized and small firms can economically create these eye-catching office brochures for client interviews, conferences, and seminars.

Joehnk Interior Design, in Hamburg, Germany, creates brochures that feature the special interest areas of the firm and an office portfolio review of recent work (figures 6.18–6.20). Pages are printed and secured with plastic comb bindings for mailing and client presentations.

A four-panel office portfolio brochure (figure 6.21) and the special project bifolders (figures 6.22, 6.23) of Atelier D'Art Urbain Architects, in Brussles, Belgium, uses brilliant pho-

6.15. CD jewel-case calendar for Nightingale Associates. 5 x 5 inches. Quantity: 1,000; cost: £1445; 2002.

6.16. Zip disk jewel-case calendar for SmithGroup. 4 x 4 inches.

6.17. Calendar for HarleyEllis. 11 x 17 inches.

6.18. Office portfolio brochure created in-house with high-end ink-jet printer for joehnk Interior Design. 8½ x 11 inches. Quantity: 1,000; cost: $10,000; ongoing.

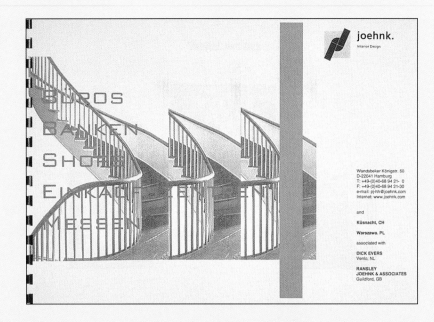

6.19. "Restaurant Design" brochure for joehnk Interior Design.

6.20. "Wellness" brochure for joehnk Interior Design.

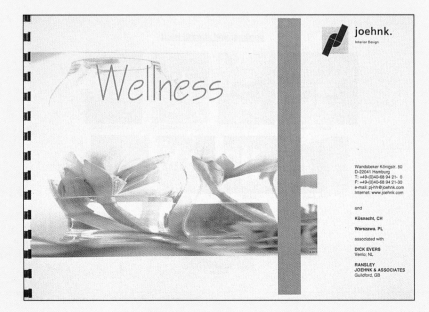

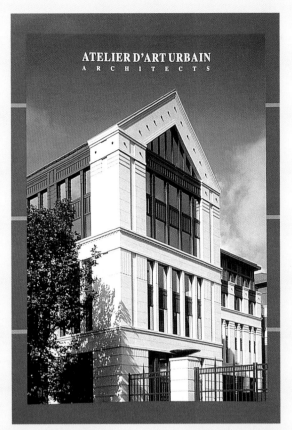

6.21. Four-panel office brochure for Atelier D'Art Urbain Architects. 11½ x 8 inches. Quantity: 4,000; cost: $9,500; 2002.

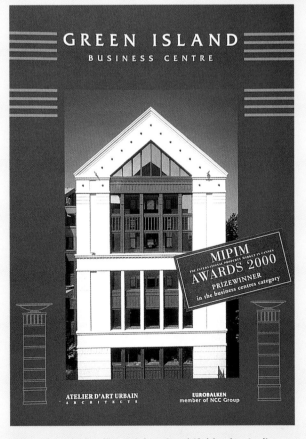

6.22. "Green Island" special project bifolder for Atelier D'Art Urbain Architects. 11½ x 8 inches. Quantity: 1,000; cost: $3,250; 2000.

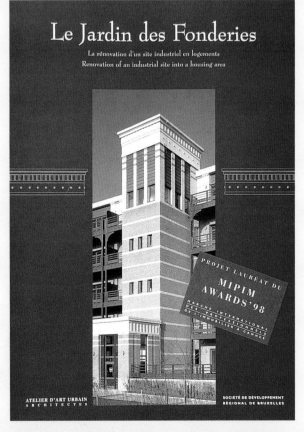

6.23. "Le Jardin des Fonderies" special project bifolder for Atelier D'Art Urbain Architects. 11½ x 8 inches. Quantity: 660; cost: $3,250; 1998.

tography and rich color to highlight the firm's capabilities and special projects, Green Island and Le Jardin des Fonderies. The graphic design format of the firm is reflected on each cover design, with bluish-green hues suggesting sustainability, and an elegant and restrained use of type.

The four-page concertina brochure of Lehrer Architects (figures 6.24, 6.25) displays watercolors created during a tour of European countries.

Specialty Flyers and Folders

Flyers and folders can be highly creative forms with innovative approaches to folding, shaping, and sizing: a single sheet can be folded in innumerable ways and then ad-dressed and mailed. Murrayolaoire architects, in Dublin, Ireland, used flyers to announce the opening of a new office (figure 6.26) and celebrate the award-winning work from each area of specialization (figures 6.27, 6.28). Designed with consistent and distinctive typography, color, and size, they unfold in panels to unveil beautiful pictures of office projects.

6.24. Folding concertina displaying watercolors of Versailles and other European sites, painted by Michael Lehrer for Lehrer Architects. Four panels, each 7½ x 8½ inches. Quantity: made to order in-house; cost: $3 per unit.

6.25. Folding concertina (open) by Michael Lehrer for Lehrer Architects.

6.26. Flyer announcement for new firm location in Cork for murrayolaoire architects. 8¼ x 11½ inches. Quantity: 500; cost: 2,735 euros.

6.27. "Education" flyer announcement for murrayolaoire architects. 8¼ x 11½ inches. Quantity: 1,000; cost: 3,192 euros.

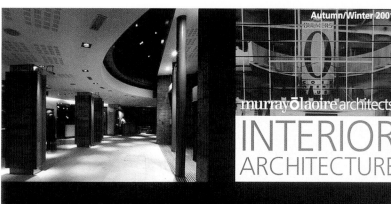

6.28. "Interior Architecture" flyer announcement for murrayolaoire architects. 8¼ x 11½ inches. Quantity: 1,000; cost: 3,192 euros.

Flyers from Loebl Schlossman & Hackl Architects celebrate the firm's seventy-fifth anniversary and history of accomplishments, and serve to create brand awareness and attract clients (figure 6.29).

Construction Sets, Banners, and Kiosks

The goal of visual communications is to appeal to prospective clients and distinguish a firm from competing offices. One-of-a-kind forms of visual communications give a firm high visibility.

Building block sets for children have held a special place in the hearts of architects. The history of architectural toys can easily be dated back to special wooden sets that Frank Lloyd Wright played with as a child and the countless variations manufactured and marketed nationally by toy companies since then. The SmithGroup has followed this tradition with the creation of a novelty deck of cards, the "Image Pack—Construction Set" (figure 6.30). Each card is printed with a SmithGroup project and is notched on all four sides for stacking into a playful construction of a house of cards. The deck is an effective handout and

6.29. Folded flyers and office brochure for Loebl Schlossman & Hackl Architects. Folded, 7½ x 10 inches.

6.30. "Image Pack—Construction Set" deck of cards for SmithGroup JJR. Each card 2½ x 4 inches. Cost: $30; 1999.

6.31. Banner for SmithGroup JJR. 3¾ x 8½ inches. Quantity: 200; cost: $4 per unit; 2001.

conversation starter at conferences and seminars and also serves as a gift to clients and friends of the firm. SmithGroup also created bold, attention-getting banners similar to those of sports teams (figure 6.31).

Large architecture firms often invest in brightly colored, attractive kiosks designed for conferences and conventions that are typically held in large halls partitioned into sections for exhibitors' displays. Kiosks generally incorporate panels of fabric or other materials with printed graphics and text, display shelves, and a lighting system (figure 6.32). The more distinctive the design of the kiosk, the more likely visitors will be to stop and browse through the literature, portfolios, and CD or DVD presentations offered there.

6.32. Exhibition display kiosk for SmithGroup JJR. 5 x 8 feet. Cost: $500.

7. Office Portfolios and Books

The traditional architecture firm portfolio is a hardbound or softbound publication, a boxed set of individual plates, or a hybrid of both the bound and boxed formats, but advances in digital technology have permitted an expansion of the form to include video and, increasingly, CDs and DVDs. The portfolio includes text and images of important resources, expertise, and accomplishments of the firm.

The traditional high-quality portfolio/brochure is generally thought of as a thick, glossy, colorful volume with many photographs and substantial text. Today design firms are questioning their value because the books are expensive and difficult to keep current, they may overwhelm clients with too much text, and they cannot target the special concerns of individual clients. The overarching purpose of a portfolio is to pique the client's curiosity and stimulate interest in a more detailed presentation.

Portfolio Contents

The office portfolio should address a firm's marketing and management objectives, specialties, or general practice, as well as its services, size, location (one city or multiple cities), departmental or project team orientation, and business structure. It should include an office profile that identifies the architects in charge and discusses collaborative project experience, special qualifications, and project management experience. It should address awards, distinctions, and business relationships with partner firms.

The following basic materials can be found in most portfolios for firms of any size.

General Summary Sheets. The general summary discusses a firm's overall professional experience and includes discussion of one or two special projects, client relationships, and the size and scope of the firm and its work. It incorporates visual evidence of the work and a basic view of the office with staff at work.

Project Fact Sheets. Each project deserves its own fact sheet. Subjects vary with the firm's work, and might include master plans, new buildings, interior design, furniture design, historic preservation, feasibility studies, research projects, special projects, product design, building system development, and so on. High-quality photographs should feature prominently in the project fact sheets. They should also include a carefully worded and concise problem statement as well as a solution statement that summarizes the goals reached and how and why the firm arrived at them. Statistics about the project, structural systems, energy systems, and perhaps some very basic costs are appropriate for these sheets.

Service Fact Sheets. Every firm offers more than one type of service. Service fact sheets may represent building types (educational, healthcare, commercial, etc.) or focus on "process services" (programming, construction management, computer software, public relations). If service generates an important amount of income for the firm, it is wise to develop fact sheets for these areas. If the income is not consequential, a listing of these activities in the general summary sheet is adequate.

Staff Biographies. Biographies tell clients whom they are working with. Individual staff members can be introduced on separate sheets or grouped according to department or team areas. Photographs are not as important as group shots, which give the client a feel for the office atmosphere in addition to introducing staff members.

Past Clients. A list of projects and clients that does not name individuals on a separate sheet promotes the success of your firm.

Past Projects. A list of completed projects conveys the range, size, and area of design specialization of your firm. Project location, dates, and brief descriptions are appropriate for these sheets. Do not include cost information, which might lead to confusion over the specifics of construction costs.

Books, Articles, and Lectures. Professional experience, public activities, and accomplishments are best represented by a list of distinguished public presentations and publications by members of the firm.

Article Reprints. Clients are interested in and impressed by what the media have to say about the firm's work. Reprints also help to connect the activities of your firm in the profession and community with prospective clients' interests and goals.

Portfolio Design

Portfolios should be divided into sections with divider sheets. A table of contents at the front of the portfolio is a must (figure 7.1); an index at the back may be useful, depending on the length and content of the portfolio.

Some designers use vellum sheets for text or visuals in addition to white paper, color stock, and cover-weight papers. Vellum can be used for section dividers inside the portfolio or as pages containing text. The material is popular because its transparency affords the opportunity to make subtle visual connections between photographs and explanatory notes or other parts of the portfolio contents. Zepeda Veraart Arquitectos, in Puebla, Mexico, and New York City, produces a portfolio edition with vellum pages for text descriptions that introduce each project in the volume (figures 7.2–7.5).

The typographic style, color, size, materials, and format of the enclos-

7.1. Office portfolio contents page for Michael Weindel, Karlsruhe, Germany. This page is organized in one-year intervals of completed projects with a showcase of selected projects and perspectives. The page can also be used as a tear sheet for introduction to a client. 8½ x 11¾ inches.

7.2. Wire-bound office portfolio for Zepeda Veraart Arquitectos. 8½ x 11 inches.

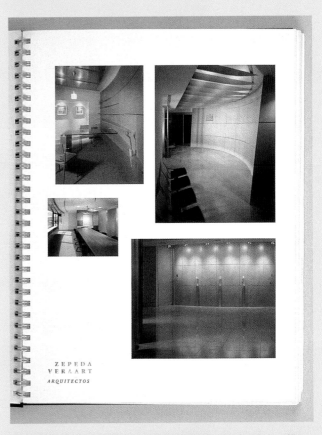

SERVICES

Planning
: Urban Planning
: Programming

Architecture
: Architectural design
: Feasibility Studies
: Programming
: Design/master planning
: Budgeting
: Specification
: Equipment specification
: Construction documents
: Construction supervision
: Architectural Planning
: As-builts
: Consulting
: Landscape Architecture

Interior Design
: Programming
: Space planning
: Interior architecture
: Lighting design
: Furniture selection
: Finish selection
: Signage design

Engineering
: Civil
: Structural
: Mechanical
: Electrical
: Hydraulic
: Environmental

ZEPEDA
VERAART
ARQUITECTOS

7.3. "Services" section of office portfolio for Zepeda Veraart Arquitectos.

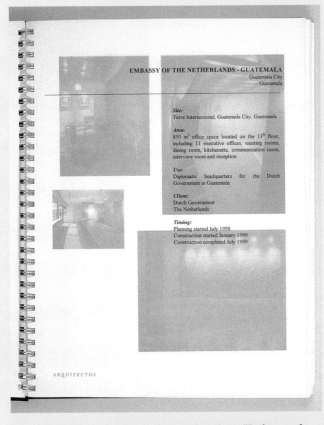

EMBASSY OF THE NETHERLANDS - GUATEMALA
Guatemala City
Guatemala

Site:
Torre Internacional, Guatemala City, Guatemala

Area:
850 m² office space located on the 13ᵗʰ floor, including 11 executive offices, meeting rooms, dining room, kitchenette, communication room, interview room and reception

Use:
Diplomatic headquarters for the Dutch Government in Guatemala

Client:
Dutch Government
The Netherlands

Timing:
Planning started July 1998
Construction started January 1999
Construction completed July 1999

ARQUITECTOS

7.4. Vellum page introducing featured project, "Embassy of the Netherlands—Guatemala," in office portfolio for Zepeda Veraart Arquitectos.

ZEPEDA
VERAART
ARQUITECTOS

7.5. Photographs of the embassy of the Netherlands in office portfolio for Zepeda Veraart Arquitectos.

ing system should correspond to the graphic design of the portfolio contents. The format can be landscape (horizontal) or portrait (vertical) and may be printed on standard-sized sheets such as 8½ x 11 inches, 8½ x 14 inches, or 11 x 17 inches, or on custom-size sheets of any dimensions.

As noted earlier, the portfolio contents may be assembled as a bound book, a boxed set of individual plates, or a hybrid form such as a combination of individual bound project booklets that slide into a sleeve or container. A CD or DVD may also be included in the portfolio.

Bound Portfolios

A bound portfolio is a hardbound or softbound printed publication with contents that are secured by a binding system that may or may not allow for removal of the pages. Bound portfolios traditionally include a cover, table of contents, and sections cover-

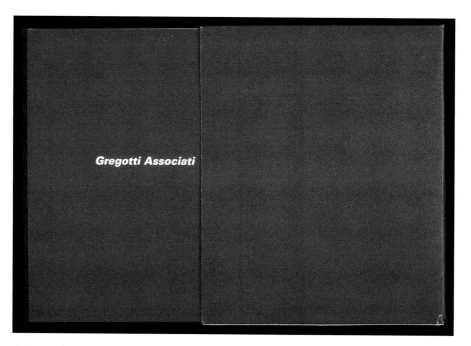

7.6. Paperback portfolio and cover sleeve for Gregotti Associati. 7¾ x 6½ inches. Quantity: 1,000 Italian version, 1,000 English version; cost: 10 euros per copy; 2001.

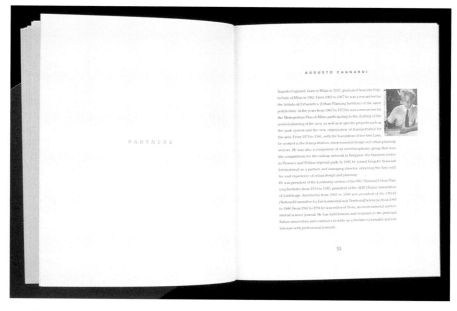

7.7. "Partners" section in portfolio for Gregotti Associati.

ing the firm's biography, an introduction to the offices and departments, staff bios, examples of office projects and accomplishments, unique qualifications, areas of specialization, awards, competitions, prizes, and directions for the future, as detailed above. There is no set limit to the number of pages in an office portfolio, but many firms include only their most current projects in their portfolios and limit the size to an average of twenty to forty pages. A sleeve to contain and protect the work can also enhance a portfolio, as shown in the example from Gregotti Associati in Milan, Italy, (figures 7.6–7.9).

Permanently bound portfolios are manufactured like books, with the pages and cover glued together at the book's spine. A temporarily bound portfolio contains hole-punched pages held together with wire, plastic, fabric, or cardboard binding coils,

7.8. Section featuring office logo and graphic design projects in portfolio for Gregotti Associati.

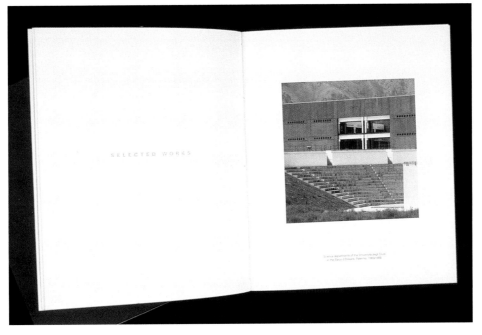

7.9. "Selected Works" section in portfolio for Gregotti Associati.

systems that allow for reorganization and the removal and updating of contents. Small binderies in most cities offer various binding solutions, and many print houses that produce portfolio pages have binding capabilities or access to nearby binderies. Note that small binderies are often the best solution because they are generally more available for the production of limited numbers of copies, whereas large binderies that produce hundreds of thousands of books for commercial publishers do not accept small orders and are rarely equipped to custom-design and fit a binding for a specific project.

Plate Portfolios

A boxed set of individual plates containing text and images is an alternative to the bound portfolio. The disadvantage of plate portfolios is that they require a more extensive investment in packaging design and construction than bound portfolios do, because boxes or sleeves to hold the plates often must be custom made. However, although plate portfolios are a complex production, they have sev-

7.10. Plate portfolio box for Ong & Ong Architects. 10 x 8½ inches. Complete boxed set (with 40 inserts); cost: SGD 52 ($30) per whole package.

7.11. Plate portfolio box (open) with office biography plate for Ong & Ong Architects.

7.12. Plate portfolio box (open) with office project plate for Ong & Ong Architects.

eral advantages over bound portfolios. Unlike permanently bound portfolios, which must be reprinted to revise, plate portfolios can be kept up to date with the addition of materials on current projects. They also allow removal of the plates from the box so they can be rearranged in any sequence for discussion, making it unnecessary to turn pages back and forth to see or compare images and text. Additionally, the plates can be removed from the portfolio and mounted in a temporary mini-exhibition or for discussion in an office or conference room. Another advantage of plate portfolios is that they can be made from a range of cardstock materials in a variety of colors and textures unavailable in papers for bound portfolios, giving you the opportunity to demonstrate a more imaginative sensibility in packaging and design.

The boxed plate portfolio from Ong & Ong Architects, in Singapore, demonstrates a rich visual presentation, with interior plates wrapped in orange tissue paper (figures 7.10–7.14). The graphic design of the con-

7.13. Plates from the portfolio box for Ong & Ong Architects.

7.14. Photographic plates from the portfolio box for Ong & Ong Architects.

tainer is in keeping with the design of each plate through a subtle background pattern in medium-gray tones. The office's orange paper disc logo is threaded by a black elastic cord that keeps the charcoal-gray cardboard box closed.

For its one-hundredth anniversary in 1995, Albert Kahn Associates, Inc., in Detroit, Michigan, celebrated the firm's accomplishments with a gala portfolio presentation—a boxed set of drawing plates, booklets, and text plates that embody Kahn's philosophy of "quality architecture that stands the test of time" (figures 7.15–7.21). The brilliant red folding box with a gold foil embossed logo on the cover contains a matching red introductory plate, and a set of mate-rials that begins with a drawing plate and then alternates between text plates (five total) and booklets (also five total), all of which are printed in gold ink. The text articulates the vision of the firm and the booklets elaborate on the growth areas of the firm's automotive, research, education, health, and commercial sector specializations.

7.15. Gold foil logo on red plate that matches the box design, with introductory text plates from the portfolio box, for Albert Kahn Associates, Inc. 8½ x 11 inches.

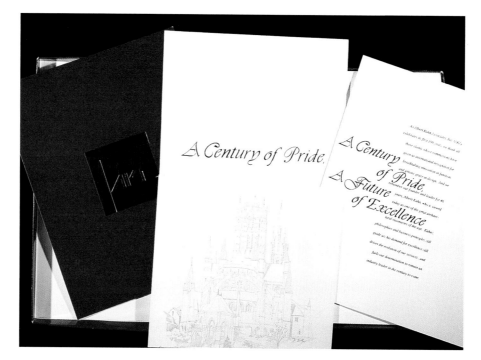

7.16. Plates from the portfolio box for Albert Kahn Associates, Inc.

7.17. "A Future of Excellence" trifolder focusing on the highlights and history of the firm from the portfolio box for Albert Kahn Associates, Inc.

7.18. Text plates discussing quality, vision, and design from the portfolio box for Albert Kahn Associates, Inc.

7.19. "Commercial," "Healthcare," and "Industrial/Automotive" booklets from the portfolio box for Albert Kahn Associates, Inc.

7.20. Trifolder and "Industrial/Automotive" booklet from portfolio box for Albert Kahn Associates, Inc.

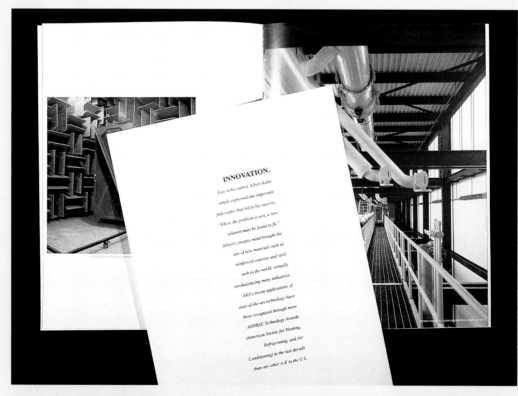

7.21. "Industrial/Automotive" booklet (interior spread) with text plate from the portfolio box for Albert Kahn Associates, Inc.

Books

Books are often used as an architectural firm's portfolio. Available in all sizes and shapes and serving a variety of purposes, they are important sales tools. They may be hard- or softcover, permanently bound volumes published by the office or in collaboration with a publishing company. The contents of office books as portfolios vary depending on the purposes of the firm. Pentagram, an international design consultancy, produced a set of unique small-format paperbacks, each with an individual theme related to environmental design projects, including lighting, monuments, architecture, and novelties (figures 7.22–7.24), that are used to showcase specific areas of design interest in the firm. The

7.22. Black Books for Pentagram. 6 x 8¼ inches.

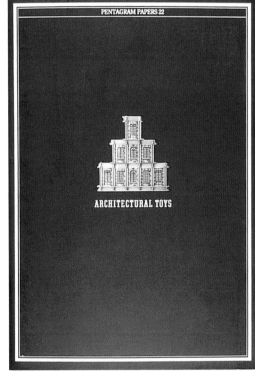

7.23. "Architectural Toys" Black Book (cover) for Pentagram.

7.24. "Architectural Toys" Black Book (interior spread) for Pentagram.

113

company also produces a large hardbound monograph that includes fifty case histories of the firm's work in architectural, graphic, and industrial design (figures 7.25, 7.26).

Six ideas about architecture, the portfolio book of eea (erick van egeraat associated architects), in Rotterdam, the Netherlands, communicates the firm's philosophy, projects,

and accomplishments through creative typographic design and page layout (figures 7.27–7.31). *Hot, medium, cool* is a smaller paperback publication that highlights their staff and

7.25. *Pentagram Book Five* monograph (cover) for Pentagram. Published by Monacelli Press and Pentagram, 1999. 8 x 10¾ inches.

7.26. *Pentagram Book Five* monograph (inside cover) for Pentagram.

7.27. *Six ideas about architecture* (cover) for eea (erick van egeraat associated architects). Published by Birkhäuser V.A. 8¾ x 11¼ inches.

7.28. Article on context in *Six ideas about architecture* for eea. Text by Deyan Sudjic.

7.29. *Six ideas about architecture* (interior spread) for eea.

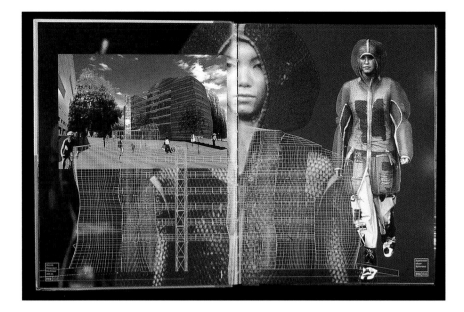

7.30. *Six ideas about architecture* (interior spread) for eea.

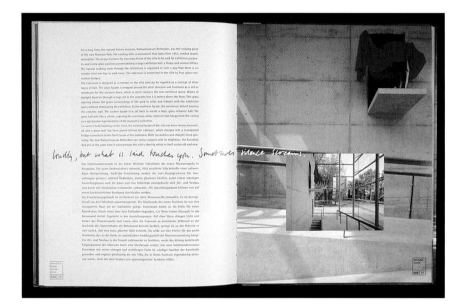

7.31. *Six ideas about architecture* (interior spread) for eea.

office projects of recent years in a playful and intriguing graphic presentation with emphasis on visual forms of color, texture, and pattern (figures 7.32–7.36).

A monograph about the partners or principal of an office can take the form of a book of substantial content, especially for firms with a long history of accomplishments like Murphy/Jahn, in Chicago, Illinois, whose *Millennium: Murphy/Jahn, Six Works* (figure 7.37) was developed by an outside author and published by Images Publishing, in Melbourne, Australia; *Helmut Jahn: Architecture Engineering* (figure 7.38) was developed in-house and published by Birkhauser in Europe.

The small publications of Fanning/Howey Associates, Inc., in Celina,

7.32. *Hot, medium, cool* paperback (cover) for eea. Published by eea. 7 x 7 inches. Quantity: 1,500 cards; cost: 1,000 euros.

7.33. Philosophy section in *Hot, medium, cool* for eea.

7.34. "Cool—Silent Forms" section in *Hot, medium, cool* for eea.

7.35. "Medium—Monomorphs" section in *Hot, medium, cool* for eea.

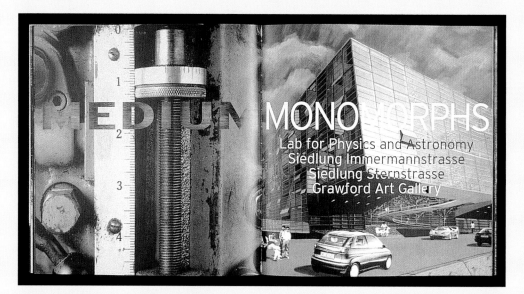

7.36. "Hot—Voluptures" section in *Hot, medium, cool* for eea.

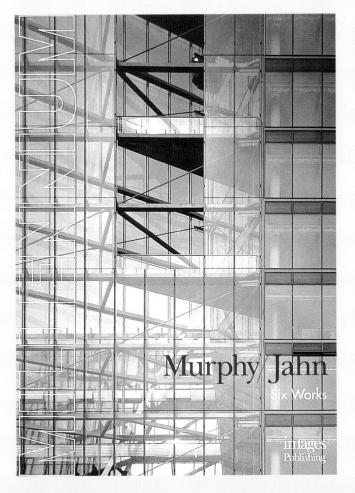

7.37. *Millennium: Murphy/Jahn, Six Works* for Murphy/Jahn. Published by Images Publishing. 9 x 12 inches. Quantity: 10,000; cost: $65 per unit; 2001.

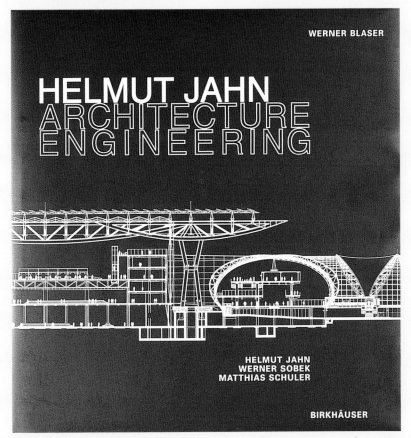

7.38. *Helmut Jahn: Architecture Engineering* for Murphy/Jahn by Werner Blaser, Helmut Jahn, Werner Sobek, and Matthias Schuler. Published by Birkhauser. 10 x 9 inches. Quantity: 6,000; cost: $65 per unit; 2002.

Ohio, focus on the special challenges and needs for the design of grade schools and high schools, an area of specialization and expertise for the firm (figures 7.39–7.41).

Books about architecture offices can also emerge from a process of discussion within the firm during which issues of purpose, image, and audience are often strongly debated. Gmp (von Gerkan, Marg und Partner Architects), in Hamburg, Germany,

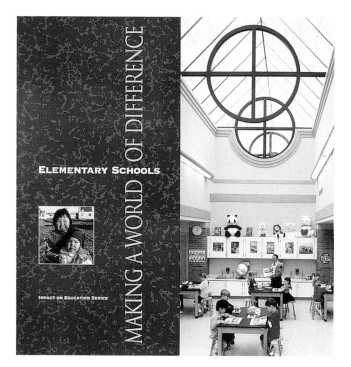

7.39. *Making a World of Difference: Elementary Schools* for Fanning/Howey Associates, Inc. Published by Fanning/Howey Associates, Inc. 9¼ x 9¼ inches. Quantity: 3,000; cost: $145,000 (including writing, design, and printing); 1998.

7.40. *Shaping the Future: Middle Schools* for Fanning/Howey Associates, Inc. Published by Fanning/Howey Associates, Inc. 9¼ x 9¼ inches. Quantity: 3,000; cost: $130,000 (including writing, design, and printing); 1997.

7.41. *Community Use of Schools: Facility Design Perspectives* for Fanning/Howey Associates, Inc. Published by Fanning/Howey Associates, Inc. 9¼ x 9¼ inches. Quantity: 3,000; cost: $120,000 (including writing, design and printing); 1995, 2001.

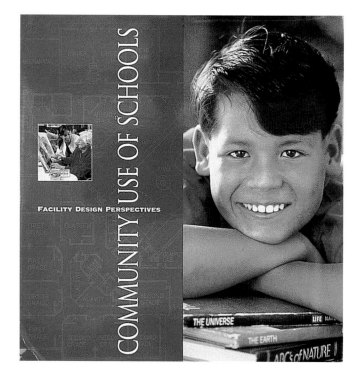

developed a series of volumes dedicated to individual projects and exciting design research directions (figures 7.42–7.44). The three paperback large-format publications are dedicated to special design projects and present the firm's research in computer visualization. RKW (Rhode Kellermann Wawrowsky), in Dusseldorf, Germany, publishes both hardcover and paperback editions of office projects. The RKW hardbound

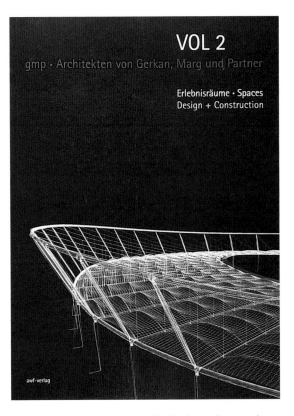

7.42. **Large-format paperback for gmp (von Gerkan, Marg und Partner, Architects). Published by awf-verlag und Autoren. 12 x 9 inches. Quantity: 4,000; cost: 65,000 euros.**

7.43. *Design + Construction (Volume 2)* **large-format paperback for gmp. Published by awf-verlag und Autoren. 12 x 9 inches. Quantity: 1,500; cost: 25,000 euros.**

7.44. *Virtuel Model* **large-format hardback on the firm's digital technology applications for gmp. Published by gmp und die Autoren, Ernst & Sohn Verlag fur Architektur und technische Wissenschaften GmbH. 11 x 8¼ inches.**

monograph of the firm's work, designed with a special slipcase, explores a broad range of office projects from 1950 to 2000 and covers awards, personnel, and philosophy in architecture, planning, and interiors (figures 7.45, 7.46). RKW also produces paperback booklets dedicated to individual projects and recent projects of distinction (figures 7.47–7.49).

Historical retrospectives are another form of publication for design firms. Dennis Lau & NG Chun Man Architects & Engineers (H.K.) Ltd., in Hong Kong, China, published a com-

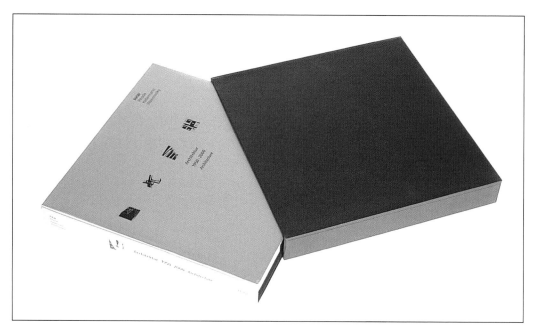

7.45. *Architecture 1950–2000* hardback monograph with hardback sleeve for RKW (Rhode Kellermann Wawrowsky). Published by RKW. 11½ x 12 inches.

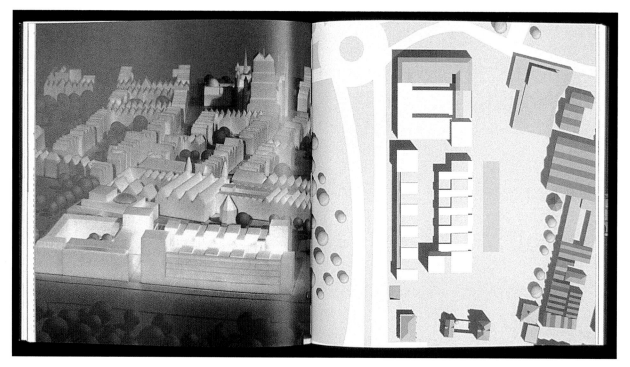

7.46. *Architecture 1950–2000* hardback monograph (interior spread: plan study) for RKW.

7.47. *KundenServiceZentrum DB Cargo* paperback booklet focusing on special areas of design for RKW. Published by RKW. 7 x 7 inches.

7.48. *2001 RKW* paperback booklet providing an overview of the firm for RKW. Published by RKW. 12 x 9 inches.

7.49. *2001 RKW* paperback booklet (interior spread) for RKW.

prehensive review of office projects over the lifetime of the firm in a handsome hardbound edition with slipcase, an excellent marketing tool with special clients and organizations (figures 7.50–7.52).

Regardless of their approach, books used as portfolios should include the elements of content discussed for all portfolios earlier in the chapter.

7.50. *The New Millennium* hardback book with sleeve for Dennis Lau & NG Chun Man Architects & Engineers (H.K.) Ltd. Published by Dennis Lau & NG Chun Man Architects & Engineers (H.K.) Ltd. 11½ x 11½ inches.

7.51. *The New Millennium* (cover) for Dennis Lau & NG Chun Man Architects & Engineers (H.K.) Ltd.

7.52. *The New Millennium* (interior spread) for Dennis Lau & NG Chun Man Architects & Engineers (H.K.) Ltd.

Afterword

Weld Coxe

Founding Principal Emeritus, The Coxe Group

If one looks at the history of marketing materials as a component of the architecture and design practice, a few things become clear: Everyone needs marketing material; less is more (or at least is enough); there is little new under the sun; and regardless of the format and content you go with today, you will probably go in a different but equally predictable direction five years from now when you update your materials.

The reason it is all so predictable is because in the three generations that architects and designers have been making serious efforts to invent a formula for marketing materials, no one has found the magic key. The reason: clients—not architects—decide what marketing materials they want and how much value they place on printed matter, graphics, and electronics when selecting architects for work. Once that is understood—that it is clients who make the rules—architecture and design firms develop their marketing materials by closely following the logical sequence of the business development process.

A look at the last century of marketing materials for architecture and design firms reveals an astounding degree of consistency. Firms communicate their credentials through a brochure or similar piece that gives credibility to the firm and can get it on the long list. Then periodicals are sent out—most frequently a newsletter or similar timely piece chiefly intended to remind clients and prospective clients of the existence of the firm (figures A.1, A.2). Finally, there are materials intended for use in interviews and related activities, when a firm is in direct pursuit of a specific project.

With the burgeoning of new com-

A.1. This anniversary poster for RTKL (Rogers Taliaferro Kostritsky Lamb Architects), Baltimore, Maryland, is a nostalgic, playful look back through forty years of the history and accomplishments of the firm. Folded, 8½ x 11 inches; unfolded, 22 x 34 inches; 1985.

A.2. "Skylines," a semiannual six-page newsletter for Blass Chilcote Carter Lanford & Wilcox, Little Rock, Arkansas, is exclusively devoted to explaining the firm's accomplishments and activities. 8½ x 11 inches; 1981.

puter technologies, many architects are experimenting with variations of digital media—DVDs, CDs, PowerPoint presentations, and so on—but we can never predict what will become state of the art in the future. What *is* certain is that once a new "state of the art" is discovered, word will spread rapidly throughout the profession and it will be widely copied with equally predictable results. The same holds true for nondigital marketing materials: Any innovation you may come up with will inevitably be copied by other firms.

This homogenization has its benefits and drawbacks. Take the brochure as an example. It is simultaneously the single most use*ful* and use*less* tool in the marketing effort. It is useful because, like a business card, it gives credibility to the practice in a way no other format can accomplish. Just envision a prospective client receiving a few loose snapshots attached to a letter, versus the same letter attached to the cover of even the simplest printed brochure. In the former instance the architect feels naked; in the latter, he or she has put on clothing. But the clothing metaphor also illustrates why the brochure is simultaneously useless: Everyone else has one too! The only way to differentiate yourself is through your choice of suit and tie or turtleneck and jeans. What's more, if you decide to wear all black at your next public

A.3. Brochure cover with die-cut reveal for Frizzell Architects, Orlando, Florida. 8½ x 11 inches; 1984.

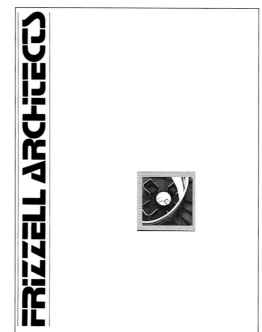

A.4. Brochure (open) for Frizzell Architects.

engagement in an effort to stand out, you can be sure that at the next interview more than one architect on the short list will also be wearing all black.

The Coxe Group, the nation's oldest and largest organization of management consultants serving architects and other professional design firms, has compiled a collection of over 500 brochures and other marketing materials created by architecture and design firms since 1933. A quick review of some of the pieces in the collection illustrates the ways these materials have changed—and not changed—over the decades.

All marketing materials are directed at clients and prospective clients and all convey the same information: Who we are (figures A.3 and A.4), what we do (figures A.5 and A.6), what we have done (figures A.7 and A.10), and how we do it.

Portfolios take the form of a series of plates compiled in a loose-leaf system (figures A.5, A.6) or a printed bound volume such as a pamphlet, booklet, or set of booklets (figure A.11).

Creative variations in shape (figures A.12–A.14), size (figures A.15, A.16), and bulk (figures A.17–A.21) abound.

The best illustration that little has changed can be seen by comparing two pieces from the collection, shown in figures A.19–A.21. The piece in figure A.19

A.5. Brochure (cover) for Reynolds, Smith and Hills, Architects, Engineers, Planners, Jacksonville, Florida. 9¾ x 9 inches; 1973.

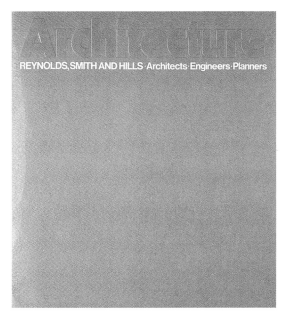

A.6. Portfolio plates showing significant projects from the brochure for Reynolds, Smith and Hills, Architects, Engineers, Planners.

is indicative of the "new" trend to publish book-long monographs intended to be sold in bookstores as well as used by firms to impress prospective clients. Its predecessor can be seen in figures A.20 and A.21, which show the oldest piece in the collection: a 13 x 17 inch leather-bound boxed portfolio of the work of Graham, Anderson, Probst and White, published in 1933. One wonders, considering the obvious investment involved and the timing of its publication (well into the Great Depression), what marketing rationale was behind its production. Nevertheless, its format and organization of content are exactly the same as every portfolio being published today. Certainly it proves that there is

A.7. Bifold portfolio with two interior pockets and two bound booklet portfolios for The Architects Collaborative, Cambridge, Massachusetts. 9 x 11¼ inches; 1976.

A.8. Bifold portfolio (open) for The Architects Collaborative.

A.9. This trifold brochure with portfolio plates for Sandlass Craycroft and Verkerke, Baltimore, Maryland, showcases the firm's projects and philosophy. 8½ x 8½ inches; 1976.

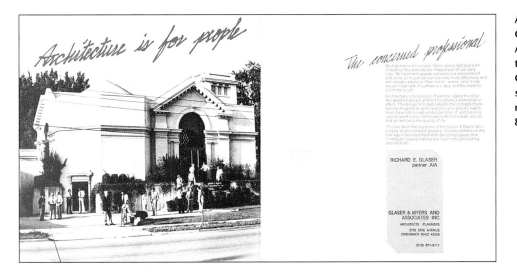

A.10. This booklet for Glaser & Myers and Associates, Inc. Architects and Planners, Cincinnati, Ohio, personalizes the firm's message for clients. 8½ x 8½ inches; 1986.

A.11. Boxed set of booklets for Dewberry Nealon & Davis Engineers, Architects, Planners, Surveyors, Gaithersburg, Maryland. 7 x 8½ inches; 1968.

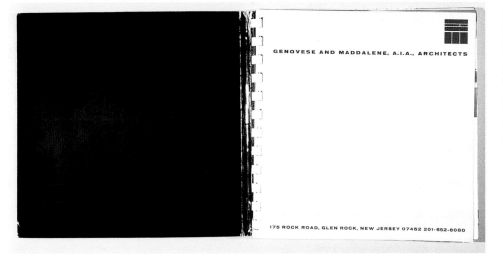

A.12. Square comb-bound portfolio booklet highlighting firm's award-winning projects for Genovese and Maddalene, A.I.A., Architects, Glen Rock, New Jersey. 7 x 7¼ inches; 1969.

A.13. Portfolio booklet (open) for Genovese and Maddalene, A.I.A., Architect.

A.14. Comb-bound portfolio booklet with large-format photographic presentation of the firm's projects for Graman Architects, Metropolis, Illinois. 8½ x 14 inches; 1972.

A.15. This large-format portfolio for DMJM (Daniel, Mann, Johnson & Mendenhall) Planning Architecture Engineering Management Operations, Los Angeles, California, includes generous visual presentations, full-page bleed photographs, and a visual history of significant accomplishments. Designed by Rosalie Carlson and Joanna Karatzas. 11 x 11 inches; 1986.

little new under the sun. Somehow, it also confirms another truism about marketing: Hope springs eternal!

Regardless, however, of the fact that everything has been done before—and that if you *do* manage to do something new someone else will soon copy it—you cannot throw out the baby with the bathwater. A firm without marketing materials is a firm without new clients.

Your goal is to create visual communications, be they innovative or traditional, that put the most accurate—and aesthetically professional—face on your firm.

A.16. Small booklet with selected firm projects for Burns & Loewe Architects, Engineers, Planners, Scranton, Pennsylvania. 4 x 6½ inches; 1972.

Neuhaus + Taylor Architects and Planning Consultants Houston/Dallas/New York

A.17. Bifold flyer with interior gate-fold photograph of a firm project for Neuhaus + Taylor Architects and Planning Consultants, Houston, Texas. 4 x 8 inches; 1979.

A.18. Bifold flyer for Neuhaus + Taylor Architects and Planning Consultants.

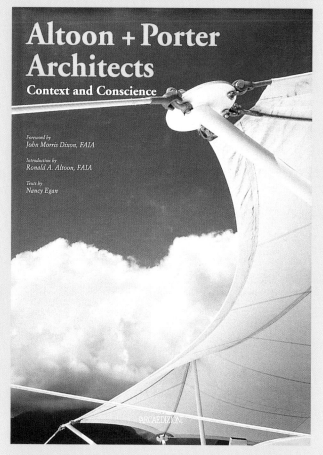

A.19. Hardbound book produced by Altoon + Porter Architects, Los Angeles, California. Edited by Nancy Egan. Published by l'Arcaedizioni, Milan, Italy. 10 x 14 inches; 1998.

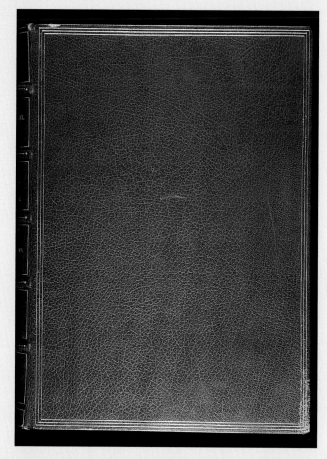

A.20. Leather-bound boxed portfolio titled *The Architectural Work of Graham Anderson Probst and White and Predecessors, D.H. Burnham & Co. and Graham Burnham & Co. Volume One.* Three hundred copies of two volumes each were published by B. T. Batsford Ltd., London, England. 3 x 13 x 17 inches; 1933.

A.21. Leather-bound boxed portfolio (open) for Graham, Anderson, Probst and White.

APPENDIX A: MARKETING STRATEGIES

Marketing strategies vary widely depending on the budget, business plan, and goals of the firm. Large firms generally work in all aspects of media and promotion, whereas moderately sized and small firms are selective regarding their use of the Internet, video, CDs, and print promotion instruments. We asked many of the firms identified in this book to describe their marketing strategies. Following are their responses.

Albert Kahn Associates, Inc. (AKA)

As one of the nation's leading architectural-engineering firms, AKA has been successful in retaining its position as the A/E firm of preference for the automotive industry. AKA anticipated changes in the marketplace and won more work in the healthcare, education, commercial, and research and development markets, which will be, forecasts current president and CEO Gordon V. R. Holness, AKA's primary markets as the firm approaches the turn of the century (figures 7.15–7.21).

Andersson-Wise Architects, Austin, Texas

The marketing challenge recently for our young firm has been twofold: first, to find the time and energy to give marketing and public relations the attention they require, and second, to publicize a firm name change.

Andersson-Wise Architects was initially established as Moore/Anderson Architects by my current business partner Arthur Andersson and the late Charles Moore. After Charles passed away there was discussion about whether or how his name should remain part of the firm name. The decision was complicated by the fact that Charles was a partner in multiple architectural firms, and our identity and individuality was at stake. It was important for us to establish ourselves independently with a view toward the future, and

we began to invest time and money into promotional materials as a rebranding campaign. Simultaneously we needed this effort to maintain continuity with our history and mentor, and that had to be imminent to the marketing materials. Our message needed to be clear to both past and future clients.

Finding the time for all this was perhaps the most challenging for our small firm, and we have found that collaborating with others is the best way to achieve our goals. Ultimately, creating successful marketing materials requires collaboration with several allied disciplines. We have worked with graphic designers to help with image, production, and a website. We have made an effort to have all our projects professionally photographed. Finally, we have recently begun working with a public relations consultant to assist in disseminating our message in a structured manner (figure 6.4).

architectus™, North Sydney, Australia

We have recently rebranded ourselves as architectus and thus there is a great need to talk to our clients about our design principles, experience, and vision. We do this in part through our corporate profile, website, presentations, and quarterly newsletters.

Marketing architecture is marketing visually. Images of our projects tell a story of design excellence. The text comes later to reinforce, back up, and expand on that initial claim. Quality is very important. Excellent design deserves excellent photography and reproduction.

Architectus aims to achieve design excellence in all projects by a consistent focus on understanding function and client objectives. Respect for place, environmental ethics, continuous research and education, and applying high-quality technology and construction standards to our work are of paramount

importance. We understand design as a process, maintaining the highest quality of design by research, innovation, communication, and review throughout the project development (figures 1.24, 1.25, 2.15, 2.16, 3.14, 3.15).

ARUP Architects, London, England

As a design firm, we believe that our marketing communications and materials speak volumes about how we view our work and others' perceptions of it. Clear messages and high-quality imagery are the key criteria that we set for success. Articulating how we have risen to design challenges and the value that we add to a client's business have a greater impact on prospective clients than "sales messages" ever can (figure 4.14, 4.15).

Atelier D'Art Urbain Architects, Brussels, Belgium

The marketing and promotional materials point up the visual and artistic aspect, the style, and the spirit. Besides these elements, an office brochure clearly sets out the way an architecture office is organized to execute its missions: its specificities, its methodology, its references, its means (figures 6.21–6.23).

BDP (Building Design Partnership), London, England

BDP is a multidiscipline practice and includes graphic designers and photographers who create our marketing material.

The *Annual Review* item has become our effective corporate brochure, backed by the Web site. We do few other print items, apart from a brochure for our retail sector, the largest of our activity areas. Each of our market sectors has its own, customer-shaped character and we encourage the leaders of that sector to reflect its style graphically and architecturally. The result across this large (800 people) and very diverse firm is that its design work is equally diverse. Only the corporate identity holds the material together visually.

BDP is not a "signature" design firm but is nevertheless devoted to design and service excellence. Our customers respond to the *Review* with excellent comments. It gives them pride to be our customers. Other collaborators respond with pleasure at being associated with us. The publication is clearly also valued internally, enabling our staff to be well informed, proud, and able to promote the firm well. This issue also marks our fortieth anniversary.

Our future policy is to deemphasize print and develop our Web site ever further. The current site is a recent redesign and has many miles to go to develop all the content it could usefully have. However, the structure is a robust one (figures 1.26–1.28).

Bentel Abramson & Partners, Houghton, South Africa

The objective of our marketing effort is to evoke the interest of potential clients and to demonstrate to the market as a whole that this company is innovative, experienced, multiskilled, and able to deliver both large and small projects on time and on budget (figure 1.23, 3.28).

Biltmore, Troy, Michigan

Biltmore Properties is a land development and building company that has been in business for over seventy-five years. Our strategies for promotion include a range of media such as Web site, print media, advertising (including newspaper), radio, and direct mail. Biltmore hosts special events that serve the community and region and bring attention to the corporation. The "Under the Stars" fundraiser for the Detroit Institute of Art raised significant funds for the museum as well as showcased new homes in the innovative neotraditional town design known as Cherry Hill Village in Canton Township, Michigan. Other events include the Michigan Education Excellence Foundation and children's local youth sports and high school fund-raising programs. In addition, Biltmore uses direct mail, radio, newspaper advertising, and a well-designed Web site for marketing (figure 4.1).

Cambridge Seven Associates, Inc., Cambridge, Massachusetts

C7A's brochure was designed as a spirit piece, or description of the firm's basic principles, with representative projects displaying our unusually diverse practice. The brochure gives a strong sense of our approach and working processes, rather than simply being a catalogue of representative projects.

Seven words were selected that most clearly described the firm's approach to design. Images of representative projects were gathered to illustrate these principles. The brochure works harmoniously with existing and newer marketing materials developed inhouse, and it organizes projects in more interesting and useful ways for our marketing approach.

Like the firm's general brochure, the exhibit brochure is meant to give clients a feeling for our design process and the diversity of our exhibit and habitat design experience, rather than being a simple presentation of a project portfolio (figures 4.5, 4.6).

Chetwood associates, London, England

Chetwood associates' success since its inception ten years ago has been built upon design innovation. By thinking laterally about each individual client project, we have been able to overcome problem briefs, meet complex challenges, and work alongside clients to unlock sites and meet their needs. As a result, we have exceptional long-standing relationships with clients and a higher-than-average referral rate.

Our overall marketing strategy, therefore, is highly focused, concentrating on niche sectors. The marketing objective is to continuously evolve our clients' knowledge and thinking, keeping the partnerships fresh and stimulating. Brochures, tailored face-to-face presentations, and e-communications have a large part to play. For new contacts, our brochures have proved to be very powerful. This is because their content aims to be a true reflection of our strengths—the application of philosophy proven in the delivery with real-life examples of built solutions (figures 5.27–5.29).

Creative Logic, Inc., Peoria, Illinois

Creative Logic, Inc.'s penchant for creative and strategy-based excellence brings the desire to produce solutions that speak directly to the consumer. Our prosperity is the direct result of our clients' success. Therefore, the best showcase to market ourselves is results-driven programs completed for our clients. We produce a series of communication vehicles and feature selected case studies included in our Web site and a unique series of well-designed booklets. These booklets highlight our work in corporate image/identity, brand development, environmental design, marketing/market research, and more. We also create clever, intellectually stimulating self-promos that our clients enjoy, are fun to receive, and show the creative problem-solving capabilities of our team (figures 1.2–1.4, 3.16, and 5.34).

Dennis Lau & NG Chun Man Architects & Engineers (H.K.) Ltd., Hong Kong, China

For any venture, but particularly architecture, with its strong visual emphasis, all aspects of marketing material convey messages. For us, the form of the message is very important, as it tells readers, or viewers, about what our firm stands for in terms of design and approach to architecture.

In content, our periodic reviews and, in recent years, our Web site have always been concise, uncomplicated, and factual. We seek in our marketing not to stand between the client and our work.

Our marketing must also inform and appeal to a very wide potential client base, ranging from multinational corporations to first-time developers, each with distinctive cultural and language preferences (figures 7.50–7.52).

eea (erick van egeraat associated architects), Rotterdam, the Netherlands

Erick van egeraat associated architects is a European architectural office that stands for an innovative and challenging architecture of high-quality standards. Specific, appropriate, and open-minded are the keywords for our way of working and communicating. We present ourselves with an intuitive and sensuous image that reflects the characteristics of our work, which benefits from fashion and design. Our aim is not to state but to relate—not to consider but to seduce, to continuously search and to react differentiated, not to irritate but to persuade and surprise (figures 1.6, 1.7, 1.22, 2.20, 2.21, 7.27–7.36).

Ellerbe Becket, Minneapolis, Minnesota

An innovator since the firm's founding in 1909, Ellerbe Becket has been a leader in architecture, engineering, and the construction industry and is a global leader in integrated design and construction of mission-critical facilities. However, mission-critical facilities have never been the hottest thing in the architecture engineering industry, and no major design or engineering firm had established ownership of the mission-critical brand. This may be due to the fact that, traditionally, high design has not been incorporated in mission-critical facilities development. Rather, function precedes form. This isn't to say that intriguing design elements can't be incorporated into mission-critical facilities. The focus simply has been on reliability and capacity.

Ellerbe Becket's mission-critical group builds more than just data centers. Call centers, control centers, web-hosting locations, and switch centers are all a part of this category. The industry's perception of mission-critical facilities changed as dot-com businesses grew in the late 1990s and demanded the reliability found in a mission-critical facility along with the finesse of a corporate office. The high-volume dot-com demand for mission-critical facilities meant short-term success, but Ellerbe Becket also wanted to drive long-term demand for its mission-critical expertise.

The key to long-term success is to visibly and publicly move into that leadership position by promoting the unique expertise and experience of Ellerbe Becket in this category. In order to establish Ellerbe Becket as the global leader in the designing and construction of mission-critical facilities, the company established a marketing communication program chartered to:

- Establish Ellerbe Becket as the acknowledged leader in the mission-critical facilities category
- Create a higher valuation for the brand
- Reinforce and expand existing relationships with Ellerbe Becket clients

Ellerbe Becket would achieve these goals using four specific tools. These include a capabilities brochure, direct mail/impact mail, CD-ROM, and e-newsletter. The results of this program in each category have proven positive and increased response rates and requests for additional materials, aided the identification of additional leads, and afforded the company customization of other practice areas within the firm (figures 2.7, 3.27).

evata, Helsinki, Finland

Evata Worldwide consists of a group of offices out of which the ones in Helsinki and Madrid are the oldest and most strongly established. In Finland, we are the largest firm in the country with a leading expertise in workplace transformation and retail and sports facilities. In Spain, our competency has been recognized in the design of shopping centers and retail outlets. From that point, our growth strategy is to consolidate our local foundations and unite our forces to develop those specific sectors on an international basis. We have been doing so both by serving our local clients in international projects and by constructing new independent relationships.

Our method is guided by our goal to provide personalized services. We meet our clients face to face, developing relationships of trust and confidence. We aim at understanding our clients' global needs and therefore being involved in projects in their infancy. In order to do so, we have diversified our services from the strictly architectural business to fields such as site finding and real estate appraisal, graphics, project marketing, and financial analysis. We organize brunches and conferences and are present in fairs in order to develop new contacts. We have also developed supporting audiovisual material and brochures in order to explain to our clients our work process, corporate objectives, design, and programming methods (figure 2.17–2.19, 3.29).

Fanning/Howey Associates, Inc., Celina, Ohio

As a leader in educational facility design, it is important to send a clear message to our clients that we are designing buildings for our children. As a firm, we have performed extensive research addressing the impact of facilities on the quality of education and have published numerous papers and articles on school design issues, as well as three books. We feel that it is essential that our promotional materials reflect our values.

Public relations director Sharon Poor is sitting at her desk flipping through a folder filled with requests for one of three books on school design that were filed on her firm's Web site. She picks up an order from a school district in Austin, Texas. "We probably won't get that job," she says. But her company, Fanning/Howey Associates, Inc., a 370-person national A/E firm specializing in the higher education and the K-12 markets, may be able to generate fees through a teaming arrangement by recommending a partner firm in Texas. "If they ask for a book, that gives me a lead, and I call to ask if they have an architect on board," Poor says.

This is just one example of how Fanning/Howey uses three books it has published on K-12 school design as a marketing tool to generate leads, revenue, and increase the firm's name recognition. "They're available for order on our Web site. We give them to school districts as a planning resource. But the main way is a leave-behind after an interview," she says.

Poor points to a $30.5 million school renovation where a member of the design selection committee said one of the books Fanning/Howey left behind was a critical factor in the school district's decision to hire the firm. That project alone generated more than $100,000 in fees, Poor says. "When you give your books to somebody it automatically establishes your credibility as an expert," she says (figures 2.11, 6.5, 6.6, 7.39–7.41).

Global, Brussels, Belgium

Our aim is to be instrumental in human and economic development whilst creating, enhancing, and simulating working environments for staff members, conducive to added value for the firm. Beyond a plain description of our business and a display of our professionalism—invariably boring to read—we wanted our presentation leaflet to reflect the enthusiasm and competence of all our staff. We have noticed that this genuine "lifestyle" magazine, which emphasizes our business, fosters the communication and sharing of our clients' core values (figures 4.16–4.18).

gmp (von Gerkan, Marg und Partner, Architects), Hamburg, Germany

Integrative Marketing Strategy (IMS) is based on the understanding that the architectural market does not exist but is generated respectively by architects.

For gmp this is an essential definition of marketing and its tools. IMS assumes that there is no nonaction, comparable to the statement by Paul Watzlawick: "One cannot not communicate." Consequently, each action of an architectural practice is a contribution to the classification, qualification, and appreciation of the architectural practice. Every employee is an ambassador. There are, for example, no bothersome or irrelevant telephone calls. Each telephone call refers to the service of the office and consequently to its competence. The architectural practice differs from the CI of firms, which are characterized by their products, such as Mercedes or a manufacturer of steel profiles, in the respect that the product to be marketed is originally an idea, a creative action, which is inseparable from the person. This immateriality makes the "product" building possible in the end.

Depending on the target group and set task, gmp develops a marketing tool that must fulfill the practice's architectural demand regarding the aspect of "visual communication." The spectrum comprises books, videos, CDs, postcards, posters, business cards, practice folders, invitation cards, exhibition and trade fairs, model photography, computer renderings, a Web site, musical events, the specific selection of locations for certain events, a representative logo, flags, signs, stamps, telephone cards and many other things (figures 3.1–3.5, 7.42–7.44).

Graham Gund Architects, Boston, Massachusetts

A firm's Web site is often its new brochure, the first impression for a growing number of people, from prospective clients to prospective employees. We often learn that building committees have extensively researched our portfolio on line prior to the RFP invitation. The site is much more than a listing of our projects: It also reflects the special culture of our office and how we work and is a tool for use by an increasingly varied audience.

Our web-management statistics have shown a dramatic increase in visits from educational servers, certainly from architectural students just entering the profession, as well as other prospective employees. Inquiries from the site have been just as far-reaching, from colleagues seeking information about a particular material or product we've used to fifth graders conducting research (figures 3.6, 3.7).

Gregotti Associati, Milan, Italy

Our main means of communication are: the newsletter (four issues per year), the institutional book, many publications, and the Web site. All these instruments are presented both in Italian and in English. The "style" of our marketing is based upon informative strictness with the greatest care of the graphic and editorial aspects in order to convey the professional qualities of the firm to our clients. The professionalism of Gregotti Associati International s.r.l. has been confirmed by almost thirty years in operation and a large number of international commissions and awards (figures 7.6–7.9).

HarleyEllis, Southfield, Michigan

The HarleyEllis marketing approach consists of three simple ideas. First, to position ourselves as experts in technically complex facilities for a select number of markets. In our case these include healthcare, science and research, automotive and industrial, civic and university, and corporate and commercial. Second, to offer the broadest range of planning, management, design, and construction services to these markets. And third, to be able to deliver our services on a regional basis through multiple offices across the country.

Each of our market studios is led by a dedicated team of planners, managers, designers, and construction specialists who focus on their particular market through project involvement and a range of positioning activities including speaking at conferences and seminars, writing articles, and serving in industry associations. Our marketing materials support these activities with a range of market-specific brochures as well as print and visual support for advertising, direct mail pieces, conferences and seminars, and proposals (figures 1.19–1.21, 2.2, 6.7–6.10).

Herbert Lewis Kruse Blunck Architecture (HLKB), Des Moines, Iowa

When we design our project-specific marketing brochure for a potential client, we create a unique piece relevant to their project. We use the same process when designing our projects: We listen (what is the client specifically asking for in the request for information?), we share (but keep the information relevant to that client's needs; we don't overwhelm them with pages and pages of information that don't pertain to that client), we comply with their schedule, and we follow through (figure 6.11).

HOK (Hellmuth, Obata + Kassabaum), St. Louis, Missouri

In 1955, HOK's founders established a vision to build a "recession-proof" practice with unmatched diversity in services, markets, expertise, and people.

Today, HOK employs more than 1,700 employees in twenty-one offices on four continents. The firm has built recognized leadership positions in several market sectors and building types, including aviation, justice, healthcare, corporate, science and technology, sports, and education. Each specialty area is represented throughout the firm's regional office network and implements its own strategic marketing program.

In the corporate sector, for example, HOK employs an aggressive business-development strategy to pursue specific clients, projects, and global alliance relationships. Marketing initiatives that support this strategy include active participation in industry organizations, maintaining a content-rich Web site (www.hokcorporate.com), and promoting the site through a postcard mailer series distributed to corporate real estate and facilities professionals. The cards feature brief profiles of projects illustrating the group's "faster, better, smarter" brand and directing recipients to the Web site for additional details. To facilitate the sharing of knowledge and information within the group, an Intranet site includes recent project news, detailed financial reports, marketing resources, benchmarking information, an industry events calendar, and a directory of HOK Corporate people.

Throughout the HOK organization, the firm's custom-developed web-publishing tools enable regional offices and business units to develop and manage the content of their own Web sites and Intranet sites. These sites are effective marketing tools for targeting specific geographic regions, building types, and specialized areas of expertise (figure 2.1).

joehnk Interior Design, Hamburg, Germany

joehnk Interior Design and JOI-Design doesn't mean design just for the sake of design. We believe in "design follows atmosphere." This means that we always target the clients of our client and try to achieve a unique atmosphere for each specific place, for specific clients, and a specific demand. Design is the tool to create this specific atmosphere—nothing more, but not less. We believe that design is a strong marketing tool in itself and helps to improve business for our clients, and by following this philosophy it helps us. We specialize in the interior design of hotels and restaurants, spa/wellness, and themed projects. This focus helps us to understand the needs of our clients. Our main office is in Hamburg, Germany, but we work throughout Europe and the world (figures 6.18–6.20).

Jones Coulter Young Architects and Urban Designers, Perth, Western Australia

Jones Coulter Young's clients are mainly public institutions, government depart-ments, and commercial developers. We therefore employ five main strategies to reach new clients and obtain desirable projects. One strategy is to respond to tender advertisements for both local and national government projects. We monitor the "property pages" in local and national newspapers and publications. We liaise with government departments for advance notice of projects. We participate in lectures and seminars for trade and industry representatives. And we build relationships with project managers who produce work for institutions and private developers (figure 4.21).

Kajima Design, Tokyo, Japan

Our firm is a multidisciplinary design organization of approximately 600 with professionals in the fields of architectural design, structural/mechanical engineering, and interior design. The image of our firm is first communicated by the office brochure, *Kajima Design*. And we send our clients the Kajima Design newsletter, which informs them of the latest firm activity, twice per year. The graphic design of all brochures, documents, and Web site is done by in-house Kajima designers (figures 1.5, 2.9, 2.10).

Karlsberger, Columbus, Ohio

Marketing materials are critical in our business. They are often the first impression and must reflect the personality and creativity of our firm. Appearance, design, and the message are all critical elements. Graphic design is integral in our architectural and interior design, which is why graphics is an in-house service (figures 2.5, 2.6, 2.24, 2.25, 4.3, 4.4, 5.25, 5.26).

KPF Architects and Planning Consultants (Kohn Pedersen Fox), New York, New York

As a rule, all marketing material, including text and graphics, must be high quality. Producing high-quality standard firm brochures is particularly critical because they introduce a potential client to the firm and play a large role in defining the firm's identity to the public. Therefore, text, including firm descriptions, design philosophies, and project descriptions, should be well written, concise, and informative, emphasizing the strengths of the firm without being overly complimentary or boastful.

Brochure graphics should reflect the design sensibility of the firm. Also, logos, text fonts, and page formats should be consistent from one promotional piece to the next. To ensure high graphic quality, the first step is to hire a talented graphic artist and skilled photographer who can help the firm build a library of project images. The second step is to compare color labs in terms of reproduction quality and prices. Using out-of-house reproduction services has proven to be extremely time- and cost-effective at KPF, but there are many firms that reproduce their work in-house and invest in top quality equipment for that purpose (figures 1.29– 1.36).

Lab architecture studio, Melbourne, Australia

Lab architecture studio's Web site aims to give visitors a sense of the design philosophy that informs all our work. We aim to intrigue, compel, challenge, and reward those who share our exploration of architecture, design, space, and movement. Our design approach proposes a reinvigorated and expanded discovery of the effects of new organizational and ordering strategies through architectural form—a laboratory of architectural speculation. Our Web site reflects this belief and encourages visitors to explore and discover. The more time someone spends with a Lab project, the more is revealed (figure 3.25, 3.26).

Lehrer Architects, Los Angeles, California

While our marketing materials are direct reflections of the firm's design philosophy, we recognize that such documents, like our firm's built work, should aspire to inspire viewer happi-

ness. Responding to continually evolving architectural technologies, building trends, and environmental concerns, the bottom line for Lehrer Architects is the application of such knowledge and responsibility to *create beauty*. As humans, we believe that beauty is a basic primal pleasure. As architects, we believe that our profession's inlet to this pleasure is places and objects that sanctify daily rituals, which makes people feel happy to be alive. It is our hope to create marketing materials memorable enough, pleasurable enough, and real enough that the recipient would want to pin them up on their wall simply because they inspire delight (figures 6.12, 6.24–6.25).

Loebl Schlossman & Hackl, Architects, Chicago, Illinois

Branding an indelible image and communicating this perception to a company's marketplace is a talent in and of itself. Gleaning a company's countless attributes and honing this cornucopia into an image that transmits definition, cognizance, and understanding is paramount to intelligent, consistent marketing. Our firm has adhered to the same fundamental principles of excellence for over seventy-five years; there is a strong sense of spirit in such an endeavor. It is this tenured wisdom of experience, inspiration, and accomplishment, combined with the vitality of youth and new talent, that must be defined, clarified, and communicated to our marketplace with strong graphic images (figures 2.4, 4.2, 6.29).

Minor Design Group, Houston, Texas

Minor Design Group opened its doors in 1987 with a few fine clients that kept us very engaged. When it slowed down, we vowed we would develop a marketing strategy. Throughout the years, the client base has steadily grown. Through good fortune, an established reputation that speaks to our process, and our close relationships with our many clients, the firm has succeeded. Our

clients have been our strongest advocates, through continued years of projects and positive promotion in the community. Marketing the firm is defined by our sincere commitment to the people we collaborate with on a daily basis and our belief in the quality and integrity of their work. We stay engaged in the community we serve. We savor any quiet moments—a time to strategize on improving what we do rather than selling what we do (figures 1.13–1.16, 4.10, 4.11, 6.3).

Murphy/Jahn, Chicago, Illinois

Murphy/Jahn has been fortunate in the interest in which publishers have shown in our forward-thinking architecture. We feel our best design approach to marketing our services is through our completed projects. We realize that we practice architecture that looks to the future, exploring design and architecture issues that hopefully lead to architectural excellence and a timeless feeling in our projects (figures 3.12, 4.22, 7.37, 7.38).

murrayolaoire architects, Dublin, Ireland

Murrayolaoire architects is a general design firm with specialist skills in areas such as healthcare, education, interiors, and urban design. Although our home market is of a size that requires us to be generalists, the international market increasingly demands specialization. In the belief that experience in one area can enrich a specialty in another area, we try to strike a balance between these poles in our marketing. While publishing our completed work in the usual way, we also try to market our work in progress by means of periodic sectored updates, as this work often embodies our most interesting ideas. Our various sectored design units market to specific sectored clients by various means— newsletters, conference presentations, and research papers. We are always looking for new ways to reach our clients and keep the material fresh—we are currently working on a book celebrating twenty-five years of work and a "customer journey" handbook, a client guide to the design process and to working with us (figures 6.26–6.28).

Nightingale Associates, Oxford, England

As architects, our business is design. Therefore our marketing literature and presentations should reflect our commitment to design quality. Our aim is to create a crisp, clear, professional identity that is consistent throughout, thereby enhancing our recognizability, both within the profession and to clients (figures 2.12–2.14, 6.15).

Ong & Ong Architects, Singapore

We believe subtle nuances tell our potential clients about what we do and how well we do it. The look of the brochure, the feel of the paper, and the weight of the package all work together to convey the same message: that we produce great designs, are thorough in all our undertakings, and are dynamic and progressive, always keeping ahead of trends and technology (figures 7.10–7.14).

Pentagram, San Francisco, California

Pentagram's structure is unique among design firms and our marketing materials need to reflect that difference. To accommodate a variety of client inquiries, we produce collateral that spans between a 500-page hardbound book featuring selected case studies to the *Pentagram Papers*, an elegant booklet format that features topics unrelated to our own work. Other items, like our small black books, are updated once a year and are discipline-specific, highlighting our work on identity, signage, industrial design, and more (figures 7.22–7.26).

Resolution: 4 Architecture, New York, New York

Resolution: 4 Architecture's marketing strategy is based on leveraging "air time." In this mediated world of the twenty-first century, getting published provides a perceived credibility. The printed word supposedly offers professional acknowledgement. Our marketing campaign begins with our postcards, a "Chinese water-torture" blitzkrieg technique of letting all of our friends, peers, and family members know we are producing architecture.

The concept being that if those close to us are aware that we are doing good work, they will "spread the word." This is a grassroots, long-term strategy that relies on the belief that we need to establish a strong foundation of perception. Our next step in the strategy is getting published. Getting published provides potential clients a type of "check mark" of acknowledgment. Get published, get published, and get published (figures 4.7, 4.8, 4.19, 4.20).

RKW (Rhode Kellermann Wawrowsky), Dusseldorf, Germany

RKW Architektur + Städtebau covers all aspects of architecture, from urban planning to interior and product design, as well as supporting clients from the early conceptual ideas, to the design development, to the construction management, to the handover of the finished project. This broad approach is reflected in the annual report, which covers the unique variety of projects. In addition RKW produces a series of small editions on specific projects or topics, such as our work in Poland or our competence in the field of interior design. Exhibitions, lectures, publication of our research and development work, and Internet activities complement our marketing efforts (figures 3.8, 7.45–7.49).

Sheppard Robson, London, England

Any medium (web, CD, brochure, advertisements, and so on) that is used as an interface between the outside world and our company must represent our culture, process, and aspirations. When we gave a working brief to our graphic/multimedia designers we tried to imagine our ideal client brief and apply those principles. We simply defined our aspirations and said there are no limits, no constraints—that's our message. Do whatever it takes to get that message across (figures 3.30–3.33)!

SmithGroup JJR, Ann Arbor, Michigan

Promotional materials for planning and design firms need to demonstrate experience and expertise that will bring benefit to the client. For this reason, we target the needs of the reader with specialty market-area brochures that primarily depend on the use of beautiful photography and interesting graphics to demonstrate the results of our work. This type of visual communication, if it is done right, can open the door for a new client relationship (figures 4.9, 5.30–5.32, 6.13, 6.14, 6.16, 6.30–6.32).

Soren Robert Lund Architects, Copenhagen, Denmark

A clear well-defined architectural vision is imperative in order to select the best-qualified architectural firm for a job. Professional presentation material combining graphic art, magazine articles, books, and interviews strengthen the architectural studio's position in the eyes of the client.

There are two ways of approaching the marketing strategy. The first is what we call the more passive. In books, magazines, and articles, clients find the studio's architecture exciting and this often leads to initial contacts. The second part of our marketing strategy is an active one. Here we use the worldwide web, where we refer to projects on our site.

Interviews are also important to our office, as they often pique the curiosity of potential clients and bring us into contact with a larger segment of the public and those who appreciate architecture.

Since the inauguration of the studio in 1991, we have taken a starting point in the vision of creating sculptural and artistic architectural expression. The design creates a sculptural exterior that is also reflected in the inner spatiality and thus creates an image where all parts of the architecture are woven together. Landscaping is an integrated part of the studio's working process. An example is the Museum of Art and the Villa L, which are both designed with an extensive interaction between exterior and interior design as a vital part of the experience. General for all projects is the contrast and combinations of materials that underlie the architecture, where especially the main construction serves as an expressive architectural element. All together the landscape, the composition, the materiality, and the spatial variations are the tools that the studio uses to create a significant architectural image (figures 4.13, 5.33).

Studio Granda, Reykjavik, Iceland

Our approach to marketing is very simple: Create architecture; the clients will come.

In addition we have three marketing devices:

1. Once a year we print a postcard that is sent to all of our clients and consultants at Christmastime. It is not sent to prospective clients.
2. Our Web site is designed in-house and is updated regularly. In addition to establishing a web presence it reduces the number of telephone calls, faxes, e-mails, and letters to those who are serious.

3. We arrange for photography of our major projects. These photographs are made available to publications on request. We do not solicit any publications (figure 2.3).

Tenazas Design, San Francisco, California

We don't have a marketing strategy per se. Most of our clients have come through word of mouth. We have a particular affinity for cultural, architectural, and design-related projects and have often been brought on as collaborators participating in large-scale projects. I am interested in the architectural design process and seek to visualize concepts behind built form in complex, esoteric, and architectonic ways. Most of the work we have done has been recognized in the design and architectural community through awards and publications (figures 1.8–1.12, 1.17, 1.18, 6.2).

TVS (Thompson, Ventulett, Stainback & Associates), Atlanta, Georgia

It is essential that the brand and corporate identity of the firm be communicated in a concise and clear manner through all of our marketing materials. Our mission is to reinforce who we are so everyone understands what we stand for and what our value proposition is. With this successfully accomplished, we stand out from our competitors. TVS promotes a collabora-

tive environment where design and marketing professionals can work together to achieve this success (figures 5.18–5.24).

Zepeda Veraart Arquitectos, Puebla, Mexico, and New York, New York

ZVA's marketing strategy is based on identifying our market sector, such as corporate, commercial, healthcare, hospitality, government, and institutional sectors, as well as identifying our client's needs. Once we have satisfied these two factors, we approach the client directly and try to fulfill their long-term goals, whether by providing a full-service delivery system or design alone. ZVA consistently strives to produce a superior product, and we are always mindful of affordability and lasting quality, which promote client activities at the highest levels.

A key to our success has been the excellence of the design team assigned to each client, with personal service always as a priority. The partners bring their experience and talents to bear on every project and the control of quality is assured by a constant supervision of all work throughout the delivery process.

Our marketing tools, whether they are personal brochures, Intranet news, publications, magazines, conferences, or seminars, allow our clients to learn about our firm (figures 7.2–7.5).

APPENDIX B: CONTRIBUTORS' WEB SITES

Albert Kahn Associates, Inc: www.albertkahn.com

Andersson-Wise Architects: www.anderssonwise.com

archimation®: www.archimation.com

architectus™: www.architectus.com

Arup Architects: www.arup.com

Atelier D'Art Urbain: www.atelier-art-urbain.com

BDP: www.bdp.co.uk

Bentel Abramson & Partners: www.bap.co.za

Biltmore: www.biltmore-homes.com

Cambridge Seven Associates: www.c7a.com

cepezed: www.cepezed.nl

Chetwood associates: www.chetwood-associates.com

Creative Logic, Inc.: www.creatvlogic.com

Dennis Lau & NG Chun Man Architects & Engineers (H.K.) Ltd.: www.dln.com.hk

eea: www.eea-architects.com

Ellerbe Becket: www.ellerbebecket.com

evata: www.evata.com

Fanning/Howey Associates, Inc.: www.fhai.com

Global: www.global-dpm.be

gmp: www.gmp-architekten.de

Gregotti Associati: www.gregottiassociati.it

Graham Gund Architects: www.grahamgund.com

HarleyEllis: www.harleyellis.com

Herbert Louis Kruse Blunck Architecture: www.hlkb.com

HOK: www.hok.com

joehnk interior design: www.joehnk.com

Jones Coulter Young Architects and Urban Designers:
www.members.iinet.net.au/~jcy/

Kajima Design: www.kajima.co.jp

Karlsberger: www.karlsberger.com

KPF: www.kpf.com

Lab architecture studio: www.labarchitecture.com

Lehrer Architects: www.lehrerarchitects.com

Loebl Schlossman & Hackl: www.lshdesign.com

Michael Weindel: www.weindel.com

Minor Design Group: www.minordesign.com

Murphy/Jahn: www.murphyjahn.com/intro.htm

murrayolaoire: www.murrayolaoire.com

Nightingale Associates: www.nightingaleassociates.com

Olin Partnership: www.olinptr.com

Ong & Ong Architects: www.ong-ong.com

Pentagram: www.pentagram.com

Resolution: 4 Architecture: www.re4a.com

RKW: www.rkw-as.de

Sheppard Robson: www.sheppardrobson.com

SmithGroup: www.smithgroupjjr.com

Soren Robert Lund Architects: www.srarkitekter.dk/indexex.html

Studio Granda: www.studiogranda.is

Tenazas Design: www.tenazasdesign.com

TVS: www.tvsa.com

von Gerkan, Marg und Partner Architects: www.gmp-architekten.de

Zepeda Veraart Arquitectos: www.zepeda-veraart.com

APPENDIX C: SMPS DOMAINS OF PRACTICE

The Society for Marketing Professional Services (SMPS) is committed to being the premier source for education and information in marketing professional services in the built and natural environment. In keeping with this mission, SMPS has conducted a practice analysis of professional-services marketing to articulate and confirm the profession's body of knowledge and skills most critical to professional competence. These knowledge and skill sets are classified under the six domains outlined here.

The domains of practice are the foundation of the SMPS Certified Professional Services Marketer (CPSM) Program. Certification is a time-tested means of measuring a professional's credentials. To earn the CPSM designation, candidates must meet educational and experience requirements, pass a rigorous written examination to assess their mastery of the domains, and pledge to abide by the CPSM code of ethics. Successful candidates are recognized as being capable of generating profitable business in the architectural, engineering, and construction (A/E/C) marketplace.

SMPS offers publications, workshops, on-line resources, and an annual marketing conference in support of professional-services marketing in the A/E/C industry. To learn more about SMPS, the CPSM Program, or the domains of practice for marketing professional services, contact the SMPS national office at 1-800-292-7677 or visit its Web site at www.smps.org. Following are the domains of practice outlined by SMPS.

Marketing Research

Sample Knowledge Areas
- Data-gathering techniques
- Sources of social, cultural, economic, federal, state, and local regulatory information
- Newspapers, magazines, and other publications related to target markets
- Research design
- Qualitative and quantitative data-analysis techniques
- Methods for forecasting trends

Skill Set
- Establish methodologies for collecting and evaluating information, from within the firm and from external sources, on potential teaming and business opportunities
- Monitor social, demographic, cultural, and economic trends for broad-based marketing and business implications
- Monitor legislative and/or regulatory activities that could affect the need for services
- Monitor sources of industry-related market information
- Develop and maintain a network of corporate, industry, government, municipal, and community contacts to keep abreast of industry, client, and competitor activity
- Design, implement, and/or evaluate research studies of markets, competitors, and/or client prospects

Marketing Plan

Sample Knowledge Areas
- SWOT (strengths, weaknesses, opportunities, and threats) of firm and personnel
- Elements of strategic plans, marketing plans, and business plans
- Techniques for facilitating the planning process
- Cost/benefits of various marketing techniques
- Basic management principles
- Internal marketing audit elements
- Methodologies for budget development
- Basic accounting principles
- Cost tracking and control procedures

Skill Set
- Analyze research data related to past, current, and prospective markets and relevant corporate experience
- Participate in the firm's strategic planning
- Select target markets based on research results
- Create a marketing plan, including specific goals, objectives, strategies, action plans, and schedules for each target market
- Manage implementation of the firm's marketing plan
- Evaluate and report progress in implementing a marketing plan and revise goals, objectives, and priorities as appropriate
- Create a marketing budget
- Manage a marketing budget

Client and Business Development

Sample Knowledge Areas
- Strategic planning techniques
- Interpreting and applying market research results to client and business development, prospect information sources
- Techniques used to screen and classify prospects
- Key elements of contact management programs and databases
- Methods for initiating client research calls and maintaining contact
- Fostering/building client relations
- Effective frequency of client contact
- Methods for conducting client perception studies

Skill Set
- Create business development

guidelines and strategies for pursuing clients or projects

• Screen or prequalify client or project leads from market research, referrals, contacts, cold calls, and other sources to establish new client relationships and to ascertain project opportunities, interest/appropriateness, and requirements of follow-up calls

• Develop, implement, and monitor contact management process

• Initiate and maintain ongoing contact with prospective clients to build a professional relationship and project opportunities

• Initiate, follow up, and maintain contact with current and past clients to track client satisfaction and initiate corrective action, if needed

SOQS/Proposals

Sample Knowledge Areas

• RFQ/RFP criteria and decision/selection process

• Fee pricing/budgeting, federal, state, and local laws and regulations

• Federal, state, and local forms and guidelines

• Architectural and engineering terminology

• Scheduling and tracking systems for individual proposal elements and status

• Graphic design and production

• Resources and production

• Resources and products for SOQ/proposal production, including printing and binding

• Desktop publishing software

• Managing activities of specialized consultants

• Presentation software

• Visual aids for use in presentations

• Postpresentation or postcontract award debriefing procedures

Skill Set

• Conduct/participate in an RFQ/RFP review and/or strategy session to analyze a potential client in terms of target market, project size, probability of

selection, and timing in order to recommend a go/no go decision

• Develop strategies to produce SOQs/proposals

• Manage the preparation and draft the content of proposals, SOQs, letters of interest, and responses to inquiries

• Produce SOQs/proposals, including typing, editing, graphics, reproduction, binding, and mailing, to ensure that all RFQ/RFP criteria are met

• Develop a presentation strategy, structure, and style and assist in selecting a presentation team

• Prepare or assemble written and visual information for presentations

• Coordinate/coach presentation rehearsals

• Conduct a postpresentation follow-up internally and with the prospective client

• Conduct postaward debriefings with prospects regardless of outcome and revise business development and SOQ/proposal strategies as appropriate

• Perform contract negotiations, including preparation of draft, negotiations, and execution of contract

Promotional Activity

Sample Knowledge Areas

• Interpreting results of client perception surveys and image studies

• Communicating firm's image and objectives

• Procedures to evaluate effectiveness of promotional activity

• Advertising media

• Business/social etiquette and protocol

• Trade show event management

• Industry/media/civic events

• Technical and journalistic publication writing techniques

• Sources for press list

• Format and content of promotional publications

• Tailoring promotional materials to target audience

• Graphic design

• Printing

• Copyright laws and authorized use of visuals

• Web page design

• Information delivery methods

• Slide production requirements and costs

• Production and use of photography

•Techniques to qualify, interview, and select vendors and consultants

• Awards programs, submission guidelines, and deadlines

• Special events planning

Skill Set

• Develop image and corporate identity

• Manage promotional program expenditures to ensure consistency with the budget

• Develop an advertising plan to support the firm's marketing program objectives

• Develop corporate entertainment strategies to ensure maximum exposure

• Represent the firm at media events, civic and professional group meetings, client industry trade associations, and community and industry activities to enhance the image of the company

• Write press releases, journal articles, and/or newsletters to generate publicity for the firm

• Create written/print promotional materials consistent with an overall marketing and business plan and update on a regular basis

• Create electronic promotional materials consistent with the overall marketing and business plan and update on a regular basis

• Create slide shows for presentations

• Coordinate finished project photography

• Select, manage, and direct the activities of specialized consultants

• Prepare and coordinate awards competition entries

• Coordinate firm special events

Information, Resource, and Organizational Management

Sample Knowledge Areas

- Management and motivational techniques
- Records management systems for project, personnel, consultant, proposal, and/or visual information
- Computerized database-management systems
- Staff training techniques
- Individual and group dynamic
- Leadership and team-building principles
- Evaluation techniques for design/production efficiency and quality control
- Promoting and rewarding high-quality team performance and effective client service
- Resource management and costs/benefit analysis techniques

Skill Set

- Manage/supervise the activities of marketing and support staff
- Coordinate marketing efforts and provide a communication link across departments, disciplines, and/or branch offices
- Develop and maintain systems to extract, categorize, and retrieve information related to consultants, personnel, projects, prior proposals, boilerplate, visuals, mailing lists, and promotional items
- Develop and maintain an internal communications program to facilitate information sharing within the firm
- Inform and involve the principals and technical staff regarding marketing efforts
- Conduct marketing-related workshops/training for the principals and technical staff
- Attend professional development activities
- Monitor information, resource, and organizational expenditures to ensure consistency with budget
- Recruit and keep star performers
- Build high-performance teams linked to key client groups
- Refine the design/production process to improve efficiency and quality control

FURTHER READING

Barr, Vilma. *Promotion Strategies for Design and Construction Firms.* New York: Van Nostrand Reinhold, 1995.

Cohen, Jonathan. *Communication and Design with the Internet: A Guide for Architects, Planners, and Building Professionals.* New York: W. W. Norton & Company, 2000.

Czerniawski, Richard D., and Michael W. Maloney. *Creating Brand Loyalty: The Management of Power Positioning and Really Great Advertising.* New York: American Management Association (AMACOM), 1999.

Demkin, Joseph A. *The Architect's Handbook of Professional Practice.* 13th ed. New York: John Wiley and Sons, 2001.

Gobe, Marc. *Emotional Branding.* New York: Allworth Press, 2001.

Harmon, Paul, Michael Rosen, and Michael Guttman. *Developing E-Business Systems and Architectures: A Manager's Guide.* San Diego: Academic Press, 2001.

Haupt, Edgar, and Manuel Kubitza, eds. *Marketing and Communication for Architects: Fundamentals, Strategies and Practice.* Basel: Birkhauser, 2002.

Jones, Rene F. *Power Marketing of Architectural Services.* Victoria, B.C.: Trafford Publishing, 2001.

Kliment, Stephen A., *Creative Communications for a Successful Design Practice.* New York: Whitney Library of Design, 1977.

———. *Writing for Design Professionals.* New York: W. W. Norton & Company, 1998.

Laermer, Richard. *Trend Spotting.* New York: Penguin Putnam, 2002.

Linton, Harold. *Portfolio Design.* 3rd ed. New York: W. W. Norton & Company, 2003.

Martin, Jane D., and Nancy Knoohuizen. *Marketing Basics for Designers: A Sourcebook of Strategies and Ideas.* New York: John Wiley and Sons, 1995.

Pickar, Roger L. *Marketing for Design Firms in the 1990s.* Washington D.C.: The American Institute of Architects Press, 1991.

Pressman, Andy. *Professional Practice 101: A Compendium of Business and Management Strategies in Architecture.* New York: John Wiley & Sons, 1997.

Richardson, Brian. *Marketing for Archi-*
tects and Engineers: A New Approach. London: E & FN Spon, 1996.

Ries, Al, and Laura Ries. *The 22 Immutable Laws of Branding.* New York: HarperCollins Publishers, 1998.

Schultz, Don E., Stanley I. Tannenbaum, and Robert F. Lauterborn. *Integrated Marketing Communications.* Chicago: NTC Business Books, 1993.

Society for Marketing Professional Services. *Marketing Handbook for the Design and Construction Professional: Society for Marketing Professional Services.* New York: BNi, Building News, 2000.

Stanley, Thomas J. *Marketing to the Affluent.* New York: McGraw-Hill, 1998.

Trout, Jack. *Differentiate or Die: Survival in Our Era of Killer Competition.* New York: John Wiley and Sons, 2000.

Webster, Bryce. *The Power of Consultative Selling.* New York: Prentice Hall, 1987.

Wind, Yoram, Vijay Mahajan, and Robert E. Gunther. *Convergence Marketing: Strategies for Reaching the New Hybrid Consumer.* New York: Prentice Hall, 2002.

CONTRIBUTORS' CREDITS

Anderson-Wise Architects

AIA Award Announcement 2001 ("Garriott Carriage House") by Kampa Design. Photography by Adam Pyrek.

archimation®

Web site design by Katrin Middel. Programming by Jens Gehrcken.

Alexander Ware, Architect AIA
Company Director

Architectenbureau Cepezed B.V.

CD-ROM by Design C III D, Amsterdam, Netherlands

Web site design by Design C III D, Amsterdam, Netherlands

architectus™

Brochures designed by Emery Vincent Design (Gary Emery Design), Melbourne, Australia

Web site design by Emery Vincent Design (Gary Emery Design), Melbourne, Australia

March newsletter by Carol Hudosn, Design/Editorial Resources, Sydney

July newsletter by alt Design, Auckland/m. arch communications, Sydney

Arup Architects

Annual Report 2001 (cover) by Arup, © Richard Bryant / Arcaid

ARUP Journal Millenium Issue 6 #2 / 2001 (cover) by Arup

Cargo Lifter hanger, Brand, Germany. Photo by Palladium Photodesign.

Atelier D'Art Urbain

Green Island designed by La Page, Atelier D'Art Urbain. Photography by Marc Detiffe.

Le Jardin Des Fonderies design by La Page, Atelier D'Art Urbain. Photography by Yvan Glaive, Celine Lambiotte.

Atelier D'Art Urbain by La Page, Atelier D'Art Urbain. Photography by Serge

Brison, Marc Detiffe, Yvan Glavie, Celine Lambiotte, Luc Wauman, Martin Wybauw, Schuco Photography.

BDP (Building Design Partnership)

Retail Design by Henrion, Ludlow and Schmidt

Annual Review by Henrion, Ludlow and Schmidt

Web site design (www.bdp.co.uk) by Henrion, Ludlow and Schmidt

Bentel Abramson & Partners Pty Ltd.

Company CV design by Nad Padayachy

Concertina leaflet design by Franc Brugman

CD-ROM design by Neil Evans

Biltmore

Biltmore bifolder. Cover illustration of Cherry Hill Village, Canton, Michigan, by Phil Hamilton. Planning by Looney Ricks Kiss (LRK) Architects, Memphis, Tennessee.

Cambridge Seven Associates, Inc.

C7A brochure design by Radoslay Mateev, David Perry

Chetwood Associates

"Pushing Ideas" design by Circle Design, London

"Sustain" design by Chetwood Associates

The Coxe Group and Weld Coxe

RTKL Architects, Baltimore, Maryland. Blass Chilcote Carter Lanford & Wilcox, Little Rock, Arkansas. Sandlass Craycroft and Verkerke, Baltimore, Maryland. Smith Chatman-Royce Associates, Paoli, Pennsylvania. Frizzell Architects, Orlando, Florida. Glaser & Myers and Associates, Inc., Cincinnati, Ohio. Reynolds, Smith and

Hills Architects, Jacksonville, Florida. Edward D. Stone Jr., and Associates, Ft. Lauderdale, Florida. The Architects Collaborative, Cambridge, Massachusetts. Caudill Rowlett Scott, Houston, Texas. Dewberry Nealon & Davis, Gaithersburg, Maryland. Genovese and Maddalene, Princeton, New Jersey. Graman Architects, Metropolis, Illinois. Daniel, Mann, Johnson & Mendenhall Architects. Burns & Loewe. Neuhaus + Taylor Architects, Houston, Texas. Finch Alexander Barnes Rothschild & Paschal Architects, Atlanta, Georgia. Altoon + Porter Architects, Los Angeles, California. Graham Anderson Probst and White Architects, Chicago, Illinois.

Creative Logic, Inc.

www.creativelogic.com design by Creative Logic, Inc.

Coffee (Photo: Rick Kessigner), Book of Logos, Design That Works, design by Creative Logic, Inc.

eea (erick van egeraat associated architects)

Book "Six Ideas on Architecture." Graphic design by Rick Vermeulen/ Mark van Beest, Martijn Bertram, Rotterdam. Concept by Deyan Sudijc, Glasgow/erick van egeraat, Rotterdam. Editing by Aude de Broissia.

Eea exhibition catalogs (title: Hot Medium Cold). Design by Erick van Egeraat, Rotterdam/Sophie Bleifuß, Berlin. Cover design by Erick van Egeraat/Folkert van Hagen, Rotterdam.

Eea project brochures design by eea

Eea Christmas card design by eea

House style designed by Rik Vermeulen

All rights reserved by (EEA) Erik van Egeraat associated architects

Ellerbe Becket

Graphic design by Ellerbe Becket/ Padilla Speer Beardsley

Evata Worldwide

Corporate brochure, retail brochures, CD-ROM design by Josee Courtemanche, Senior Project Manger and Chief Graphic Designer

Fanning/Howey Associates, Inc. (Architects, Engineers, Consultants)

Elementary Schools (book) design by Capstone Communications, Capitol Design, Inc.

Middle Schools (book) design by Capstone Communications, Capitol Design, Inc.

Facility Design Perspectives (book) design by Capstone Communications, Capitol Design, Inc.

Higher Education Services flyers design by Capstone Communications, Capitol Design, Inc.

TVS bifold office folder design by Capstone Communications, Capitol Design, Inc.

Award Citations 2001 design by Capstone Communications, Capitol Design, Inc.

Global (Design Project & Facility Management)

Global Edition 2002 by sdesign, Johanna Fischer

Gmp-Architekten, Germany

Books:
von Gerkan, Marg und Partner, Architecture 1999–2000 graphic design by Dominique Oechsle, Hamburg

VOL 2. Erlebnisräume—Spaces. Design + Construction graphic design by Birgit Meyer and Bernd Pastuschka, gmp, Hamburg

modell virtuell graphic design by ON Industriedesign—Andreas Ostwald, Klaus Nolting, Tom Wibberenz. Idea and concept by Bernd Pastuschka.

Videos:
New Trade Fair, Leipzig cover design by Birgit Meyer, gmp, Hamburg

The "Red Wonder" cover design by Birgit Meyer, gmp, Hamburg

CDs:
Meinhard von Gerkan und Volkwin Marg erzählen: Geschichten aus 40 Jahren einer gemeinsamen Profession graphic design by Real Dreams, Hamburg

modell virtuell graphic design by Thomas Nowack, Dominique Oechsle, Bernd Pastuschka, Hamburg

Digital business card. CD cover and booklet by Birgit Meyer, gmp, Hamburg. Realization of CD by Macina, Hanover. Idea and concept by Bernd Pastuschka.

Gregotti Associati Int. S.R.L.

Office brochure. Graphic design by Andrea Lancelloti. Text by Bruno Pedretti. And by Gregotti Associati International, Milan, Venice.

Examples of publishing graphics, logos, and exhibition layout designs 1976/1996 design by Gregotti Associati International

Science Departments, University degli Studi in the Parco d'Orleans, Palermo 1969/1988, photography by Mimmo Jodice

Graham Gund Architects

GGA Web site by Carlos Ridruejo

HarleyEllis Architects

College & University Sector brochure by HarleyEllis Design

Science & Research Sector brochure by HarleyEllis Design

Automotive & Industrial Sector brochure by HarleyEllis Design

Reflections 2000 CD-ROM by HarleyEllis Design

Reflections 2000 CD-ROM (inside view) by HarleyEllis Design

Firm of the Year 2000 (mailer) by HarleyEllis Design

Alphabet postcards by HarleyEllis Design

New Office Announcements (Cincinnati) by HarleyEllis Design

Herbert Lewis Kruse Blunck Architecture

"No Jacket Required" design by HLKB Architecture

HOK

Faster, Better, Smarter postcards by HOK

Joehnk Interior Design

Office Portfolio and Hotel Sector booklet by Joehnk Interior Design

Jones Coulter Young Architects & Urban Designers

5-year JCY Office brochure. Photography by Patrick Bingham-Hall. Graphic design by Kirk Palmer Design, Sydney, Australia.

Kajima Design (architectural & engineering design division)

Kajima Design, Vol. 8. by Kajima Design. Hotel Monteray Nagasaki photograph by Satoshi Asakawa. Kajima Corporation Minaminagasaki Dormatory photography by KAPO.

Kajima Design newsletter (Vols. 8, 9, 10) by Kajima Design

Karlsberger

Karlsberger Planning Group (four-panel folder) design by Karlsberger Graphics Group

Choices, Questions, Solutions (cards) design by Karlsberger Graphics Group

Karlsberger Laboratory and Technology Group brochure design by Karlsberger Graphics Group

Karlsberger "Cool People" brochure (cover) design by Karlsberger Graphics Group

Kohn Pedersen Fox Associates PC

Graphic design by Kohn Pedersen Fox Associates PC

Lab architecture studio

Web site design by CPD Media, New South Wales, Australia

Federation Square design by Lab architecture studio in association with Bates Smart

Federation Square photography by Trevor Mein

Photography of Berlin exhibition by Lab architecture studio

Berlin Arch Workshop designs by Narczik and Neffe

Dennis Lau & NG Chun Man Architects and Engineers Ltd.

"The New Millenium Company Review" by Dennis Lau & NG Chun Man. Photography by Mr. Frankie F. Y. Wong.

Lehrer Architects

Lehrer poster design by Lehrer Architects

Woods Community Center graphic design by Lehrer Architects

Downtown Drop-in Center design by Lehrer Architects

LehrerArchitects.com design by Christopher Mundweil, Lehrer Architects, and Nerin Kadribegovic

Watercolors on concertina office flyer design by Christopher S. Mundweil

Loebl Schlossman & Hackl

Firm brochure graphic design by Sara Van Nuland & Michael Romane

Newsletter by Connie Garrison, Editor

Anniversary pieces by Sara Van Nuland and Connie Garrison

Soren Robert Lund, Architect

Soren Robert Lund Architects 2002 (brochure) design by Laura Juvik

Arken Museum of Modern Art photograph by Christina Capetillo

Colt Telecom photograph by Soren Robert Lund

Minor Design Group

Synectics Group, The Office of James Burnett, Ray + Hollington, Murphy Mears Architects, Linda Sylvan (Rice University) design by Minor Design Group

Murphy/Jahn Architects

"Murphy/Jahn Millennium Series," The Images Publishing Group Pty Ltd, 2001

"Helmut Jahn Architecture Engineering," by Birkhäuser Verlag AG, 2002

"Helmut Jahn–Extra Edition," A + U Publishing Co., Ltd., 1986

"Helmut Jahn 1982–1992," A + U Publishing Co., Ltd., 1992

"Hotel Kempinski," A + U Publishing Co., Ltd., 1995

Web site design by Murphy/Jahn

Towers and Current Works (office brochures) design by Murphy/Jahn

Messeturm Tower (Towers) design by Murphy/Jahn

Sony Center Berlin (Current Work) design by Murphy/Jahn

murrayolaoire architects

Interior Architecture Review, Education Sector Review, Cork Opening office newsletter, and MOLA calling card design by murrayolaoire architects

Nightingale Associates Architects

Calendar 2002 in jewel case, holiday cards, Oxford Program brochure and guest list, and invitation and office notes design by Catherine Nightingale, Nightingale Associates

Olin Partnership Ltd., Landscape Architecture, Urban Design

The Olin Partnership 25 Year Book/Portfolio by Thinkframe

The Olin Partnership brochure by Barbara McGrath, McGrath Design

Ong & Ong Architects

Office box plate portfolio by Ong & Ong Architects PTE LTD

Pentagram

Pentagram Book Five, Pentagram supplements (New Stops–Granada Motorway), Pentagram supplement (Bus Shelters), Pentagram supplement (Rebuilding Shakespeare's Globe), Black books (Savoy Lights, Reading With a Purpose, Lets Build a Monu-

ment, Architectural Toys, Pentagram Signs), and Architectural Toys (Town and Castle, City Building Blocks) design by Pentagram Design

Philips Swager Associates Architects (PSA)

First Prebyterian Church Interview booklet

Interview presentation boards

Resolution: 4 Architecture

Resolution: 4 Architecture—An Idea of a Site Text (book) published by l'Arcaedizioni. Downtown Suffern (aerial view model with plans & perspectives).

Postcards design by principals Joseph Tanney & Robert Luntz.

Interior Design Magazine and Interiors Magazine reprints: Light Box: Tribecca loft (Paul Warchol). McCann-Erickson 16th Floor (Eduard Hueber/Arch Photo).

RKW (Rhode Kellermann Wawrowsky) Architektur + Städtebau

Architektur 1950–2000 published by Velag Gerd Hatje. Design by Felix Busch, Sandra Balke. Logos by kommunikation und Gestaltung Wuppertal. © 1998 Verlag Gerd Hatje, Ostfildern-Ruit, die Autoren und Fotografen.

Polska 1999–2001 RKW.KundenServiceZentrum DB Cargo Duisburg RKW. Design by RKW Rhode Kevermann Wawrosky Architektur + Stadtebay hd schellnack, nodesign.

2001 RKW booklets design by RKW Rhode Kevermann Wawrosky Architektur + Stadtebay hd schellnack, nodesign

Web site design by RKW Rhode Kellermann Wawrowsky) Architektur + Städtebau

Sheppard Robson

Office portfolio (bifold brochure and CD-ROM brochure) design by S.R./Attik

Toyota brochure design by S.R./Attik

Interior spread (Toyota brochure) design by S.R./Attik

Sector brochures & CD-ROM package design by S.R./Attik

Gary L. Skog, FAIA HarleyEllis Architects

Frontmatter by Gary L. Skog, FAIA Harley Ellis Architects

SmithGroup

Calendar in jewel case

Image Pack—Construction Set

SmithGroup JJR

Four-panel brochure, announcements by SmithGroup JJR

"Cities & Communities," "Waterfronts," by SmithGroup JJR

CD-ROM bifold cover by SmithGroup JJR

"Landscape Architecture" brochure, "Urban & Regional Planning" brochure by SmithGroup JJR

Banner by SmithGroup JJR

Urban Spaces 2 by Visual Reference Publications, Inc.

Society for Marketing Professional Services

Are you looking for new ways to improve your bottom line? brochure design by Frost Miller Group

Are you ready to take your career to the next level? brochure design by Frost Miller Group

Studio Granda

Studio bifold card and office project cards by Steve Christer, Studio Granda

Tenazas Design

Logo design and identity system, Client: SMWM, an architecture, interiors and planning firm based in San Francisco renowned for the public spirit of its work. Projects include The San Francisco Main Public Library and the Massachusetts Turnpike Authority. Creative Director: Lucille Tenazas. Senior Designer: Brett McFadden.

Marketing brochure. Client: Baum Thornley Architects. Creative Director/Designer: Lucille Tenazas.

Logo design and identity system. Client: Ross Drulis Cusenbery Architecture. Creative Director: Lucille Tenazas. Senior Designer: Zaldy Serrano.

Logo design and identity system. Client: Levy Design Partners. Creative Director: Lucille Tenazas. Senior Designers: Zaldy Serrano Kelly Tokerud Macy (folder design).

Logo design and identity system. Client: Gordon H Chong & Partners Architecture. Creative Director: Lucille

Tenazas. Senior Designer: Kelly Tokerud Macy

AIA San Francisco Lecture Series. Clients: AIA SF/SFMoMA. Creative Director: Lucille Tenazas. Designers:1996 Kelly Tokerud Macy. 1997 Kelly Tokerud Macy. 1998 Richard Leighton. 1999 Richard Leighton. 2000 Zaldy Serrano.

TVS (Thompson, Ventulett, Stainback & Associates, Inc.)

AIA 2002 Architecture Firm Award (concertina & envelope) design by TVS

TVS Interiors brochure by TVS

TVS Corporate brochure design by Iconologic

International China Marketing Materials by TVS

Photography: Brian Gassel, TVS

Michael Weindel Architect

Office brochure design by Michael Weindel. Photography by Ivan Nemec, Frankfurt + Berlin, Germany, and Angelo Kaunat, Graz, Austria.

ZVA Arquitectos (Zepeda Veraart Arquitectos)

ZVA portfolio design by Lorena Plata

Embassy of the Netherlands photography by Victor Benitez

INDEX

Page references in *italic* type refer to figures.